ELEMENTAL LEADERS

Four Essentials Every Leader Needs
...And Every Church Must Have

INTEGRITY | PASSION
SERVANTHOOD | IMAGINATION

DAVE WORKMAN

ACKNOWLEDGEMENTS

Literally dozens of people read this manuscript leading to numerous changes—gracias to all who critiqued, supplemented and added value. A special debt of gratitude is due my comrade-in-arms Tom Thatcher who wrote the fabulous accompanying Field Guide. Props to Al Buchweitz, Molly Zakrajsek, Brian Harkness, Tom Heuer, Dave Vercellino, J.R. Cifani, Steve Cesler, Bill Brown, Susan Fuchtman, Geoff Mandeville, and Jason Clark (who planted the seed), all of whom encouraged, raised questions and pointed out holes in the plot. I'm grateful for all the churches who let me beta test and hone this material over the years. Thanks to Ron Heineman for your investment—I'm deeply appreciative. Last, I'm indebted to the Elemental Churches team for your friendship and commitment to helping organizations grow better. Together.

For Anita.
Wise wife, best friend,
and first-rate elemental leader.

ELEMENTAL LEADERS
Four Essentials Every Leader Needs
...And Every Church Must Have

CONTENTS

INTRODUCTION: a personal struggle with leadership...and leading

First, a confession: I'm a classic reluctant leader. Years ago I wrestled quite a bit with whether I had the right stuff or if I had any leadership genes. But while I might consider my baptism into leading as "kicking and screaming," a little reflection has caused me to rethink that a bit. My journey began in high school in the 1960's as part of a counter-cultural reaction to what we considered the tone-deaf status quo of the American establishment. It was a rapidly changing country mired in racial inequality, with thousands of body bags returning from Vietnam during a questionable war with a military draft of boys old enough to carry bazookas but too young to vote, women who were frustrated with disparity and few opportunities in a condescending man's world, and a gaping chasm between generations over shifting mores.

Long hair and Afros were the passwords to a burgeoning underground movement even as billboards sprang up across the landscape with a "we-don't-like-you" message: *Beautify America: Get a Haircut.* In solidarity, we wore black armbands on Moratorium Day and risked expulsion growing our hair in schools with strict dress codes. It was perhaps less about style and more about identification with a movement. I was reading *Catch-22, Johnny Got His Gun* and other antiwar books at the time while experiencing rejection and physical threats simply because of the way I looked.

But I somehow found myself as a shy, skinny teenager attending school board meetings, addressing the student body, and drawing stinging editorial cartoons for the school newspaper. I never saw myself as a leader, but a teenager

1

troubled by what seemed to me blatant justice issues and societal ills.

And then after dropping out of college while working as a professional musician, I had an encounter with the Holy Spirit via the Jesus movement. I didn't know it, but I was ripe for inner change, for a heart transplant. Even though as a generation we were advancing our cause for cultural change, the waters were muddy with drugs, promiscuity, and hypocrisy while media and advertisers kowtowed to us. These were heady days, and into that confusing swirl came a move of the Holy Spirit that swept across the globe.

It soon became obvious to me that using music as a cultural connector, especially for my generation, was the way to introduce the radical, life-transformational message of Jesus, the itinerant Jewish healer and preacher from a backwoods town who made outrageous claims in his own behalf.

After crisscrossing the country for years in a Jesus-rock band and three vinyl albums later (remember those?), I stumbled into a house church with priorities that seemed to match my sensibilities: let's worship God simply, authentically build community and take care of the poor. I had discovered my tribe. Our founder and father of servant evangelism, Steve Sjogren, had created a beautiful DNA for the future. After a four-year slow start, we suddenly began to grow like crazy.

A decade-and-a-half later, I entered into the senior pastor role. Over the next thirteen years, we continued to grow with a fantastic team eventually overseeing a volunteer army of thousands, a staff of over a hundred people and a weekend attendance of six thousand people, doubling our budget over the next decade. After directly and indirectly planting dozens of other churches in the area, we opened a multi-million dollar facility called the Healing Center, a non-profit on our campus in the north side of Cincinnati to serve thousands of people every month with over forty different services requiring a crew of five-hundred volunteers, taking a holistic approach to meeting the needs of people—the poor and poor in spirit—in our city. We simultaneously launched the H_2O Nigeria Project that would drill over a hundred water wells throughout the Plateau state of the most populated country in Africa. We had become a complex, multilayered organization.

Our church was powerfully challenged by Jesus' missional words:

> *"The Spirit of the Lord is on me, because he has anointed me to preach good news to the poor. He has sent me to proclaim freedom for the prisoners and recovery of sight for the blind, to release the oppressed, to proclaim the year of the Lord's favor."* [1]

It seemed to us that we had a clear mandate from God. We had never taken a fortress or defensive stance regarding the relationship between church and culture, but rather a gentle, servant-hearted approach, reminiscent of the words of the prophet Jeremiah during Israel's exile,

> *"...do good things for the city where I sent you as captives. Pray to the LORD for the city where you are living, because if good things happen in the city, good things will happen to you also."* [2]

And now, after helping lead our own senior pastor transition, I find myself reflecting on the leaders I've admired and followed over many years, my own successes and failures, as well as resources from an insatiable curiosity about leader-

---

[1] Luke 4:18-19
[2] Jeremiah 29:7 (New Century Version)

ship, noted by bulging bookshelves and a maxed out tablet on leadership literature. This is more than a passing interest; as a practitioner and student, I'm mesmerized by the symbiosis of spiritual maturity, character, gifting and competency in the context of leading others, particularly in the Kingdom of God. *Lead with all diligence* [3], as the Apostle Paul admonishes.

As of this writing, I've been following Jesus for over forty years. He is the ultimate leader, the one to whom I've pledged allegiance and followership for decades. For me, he exemplifies the four absolutely essential elements of leadership: Integrity, Passion, Servanthood and Imagination.

Or for our mnemonic: Earth, Fire, Water and Air. Four must-haves for Elemental Leaders.

Dave Workman, 2016

---

[3] Romans 12:8

CHAPTER 1
THE FOUR ELEMENTS OVERVIEW

This is a simple book on leadership. It's written for people who want to lead anything well, from a family to a team to a complex organization. But let me warn you: because something is simple doesn't mean it's easy. Let's get that out of the way quickly. The danger for readers (and writers) of books bordering on *how-to* is confusing simplicity with ease.

For instance, if the premier premarital tip for a healthy marriage is communication, ask someone who's been married for more than five years if the give-and-take of words and thoughts comes easy.

Or consider this: the point of American football is simple—end up on the other side of a goal line with a leather oblong ball. But tell the wide receiver who's leaping three feet vertically to pull in a poorly placed pass while a one-hundred-eighty-pound safety is barreling at him full bore that all he has to do is catch-and-grab and stretch for a first down.

And tell the film score songwriter that all she needs to do is write a powerful emotive melodic ballad of unrequited love for a dramatic turning point in the romantic comedy that's waiting for her creative voice.

Simple doesn't equal easy.

But certainly not impossible. Leaders aren't born, they're developed as long as they get good tools, have skills modeled for them and are given opportunities. The scope of their leadership may vary, but they can be developed.

After decades of leading in various capacities and observing leaders as a follower, I've come to believe that effective leadership could be boiled down to four basic factors, what I call elemental leadership. For the sake of simplicity and retention, I use the four foundational elements that the ancient Greeks reduced the world to: Earth, Fire, Water and Air.

THE ELEMENTAL LEADER

Earth | Integrity

There's something solid, rooted and grounded in the elemental leader's character. What's more, they build a similar integrity in the organizations they lead. They are driven by principles and values and a deep desire for praxis in their personal lives, their teams, their organizations and their practices.

Fire | Passion

This catalytic element fuels inspiration and energy; elemental leaders bring heat to others and situations in order to enable things to combust. Things happen. Every successful leader I've known had a fire in their belly for a mission that ignited in others a sense of empowerment and a longing for accomplishment. That doesn't mean they have a salesperson-type personality or are extreme extroverts. But it does mean they have to be able to express that inner-passion for a particular purpose in some contagious way.

Water | Servanthood

Elemental leaders deeply understand that the organization (or family or team) is not about them—as a matter of fact, it's more important than oneself. Elemental leaders innately grasp they're part of something bigger than themselves. They regularly fight with and shake off any sense of entitlement, giving life rather than expecting it. They are outward-focused and feel as though they are being poured out. Many leaders with a Water|Servanthood orientation have grown up in the organization.

Air | Imagination

There's a certain amount of blue sky-ing elemental leaders enjoy with their teams and leaders. They have no problem grilling up sacred cows or questioning organizational methodologies. There's a "what-if" factor that fires their neurons regularly and a certain amount of calculated risk that cultivates organizational "room-to-breathe."

Of course, no leader is perpetually functional in all four areas, but learn to recognize and compensate for the gaps as well as make themselves accountable to the people they lead for all four elements to thrive in their organization. They exercise the weak muscles. Highly functioning leaders learn how to balance all four in ways that feel semi-predictable yet surprisingly intuitive and fresh to their organizations and followers. They learn to situationally recognize why and when one of the elements needs to be amped up.

EARTH | INTEGRITY:
solid; interdependent; holistic

FIRE | PASSION:
energizing; inspirational; activistic

WATER | SERVANTHOOD:
life-giving; others-first; poured-out

AIR | IMAGINATION:
blue-sky thinking; innovative; creative

THE ELEMENTAL ORGANIZATION

Healthy organizations can be characterized by these same four key traits: Integrity, Passion, Servanthood, and Imagination. While each of these is significant in its own right, and while different organizations may naturally excel at some more than others, all must be present and effectively balanced. From an *organizational* perspective, the four elements are expresses thusly:

Earth | Integrity

Systems and processes are present, functional, and effective toward achieving goals. An organization with integrity has a clear sense of mission and purpose, and maintains systems that leverage resources toward accomplishing its goals.

Fire | Passion

People within the organization support and are engaged in the mission. They understand the vision and are energized toward helping the organization reach its goals. A widespread sense of ownership is evident.

Water | Servanthood

The organization, and individuals within it, demonstrates an outward focus. Energy is invested in the larger mission, not in personal success; a spirit of teamwork is evident, and individuals don't think and act from a sense of entitlement. The organization at large is concerned about the needs of those it seeks to reach, not about its own history and survival.

Air | Imagination

The organization can envision possibilities that transcend past and present realities. Individuals are open to new possibilities, and innovation is rewarded. Change is not undertaken for the sake of change, but rather for sake of remaining relevant and effective.

Even before we unpack these elements throughout the following chapters, I'll venture you already have a sense that one of those elements is currently atrophied in whatever setting you lead. Or perhaps even in your own leadership. Is there a lack of passion or fire in your church...your family...your team? Or does it seem like it's been a long time since creativity played any part in the strategy, structure or processes of your church, ministry or company? Or has a cancerous negativity or unhealthy entitlement crept into your staff, co-workers, team or family?

We can all learn to lead in healthy ways that foster growth, both personally and for our organizations in whatever ways you measure health and success. Although this is a book about leadership and organizations in a spiritual context and leans into the life of the one I trust and follow as my leader, Jesus of Nazareth, I think anyone will find the principles sound, universal and, hopefully, more than a little helpful.

CHAPTER 2
EARTH | INTEGRITY

Love and truth form a good leader; *sound leadership is
founded on loving integrity.*

~PROVERBS 20:28 (THE MESSAGE)

O ver the years I've admired those leaders who seemed rooted and grounded in who they were. To put it simply, it was as if their walk and their talk were fully synchronized. They were solid and trustworthy and their emotional intelligence and self-awareness were integrated with their competencies and character.

The simplest word for this kind of wholeness is integrity.

Integrity is rooted in the Latin word *integer*, which means a whole number in mathematics. It implies that something is "whole" or "all in one piece" and that everything is integrated into *one*.

Throughout the Bible, the word one is important. God told Moses to repetitively teach Israel the shema: *"Hear O Israel: the Lord our God, the Lord is one."* [4] It meant that God was perfectly whole and integrated within himself. That's why Jesus said, *"I and the Father are one."* [5] He meant that they were complete as one. Or as he put it, *"If you've seen me, you've seen the Father."* [6]

Even our English word *holy* is rooted in this idea of whole or wholeness and oneness. [7] When God told Israel to *"be holy even as I am holy,"* [8] there was a lot more to it than adherence to a list of rules. They were to be integrated with God's purposes and character. When they weren't operating with integrity, they were said to be profaning God's name [9] and breaking the oneness they had with God.

Likewise, elemental leaders understand the power of integrity, not only personally but within the organizations and

---

[4] Deuteronomy 6:4
[5] John 10:30
[6] John 14:9
[7] The word *atone* simply means as it's spelled out: *at one*. *Atonement* means our sins have been dealt with and we are *at one* with God; we finally have integrity with God.
[8] Leviticus 19:2
[9] Ezekiel 36:20

teams that they lead. They recognize the critical nature of "organizational oneness."

THE ORGANIZATIONAL INTEGRITY TRIANGLE

Typically, when we talk about integrity we default to only thinking about it at an individual level. But organizations must be built with integrity as well. In architecture, the triangle is understood to be the strongest structural shape; likewise with what I call the *Organizational Integrity Triangle*. The health and effectiveness of any organization depends on the strength of each of the points of the triangle.

In the *Organizational Integrity Triangle* model, we find three simple, critical structural components: Personal, Missional and Systemic Integrity. If any one of those breaks down, the church—or any organization—will collapse. An effective leader will be paying attention to these three components on a regular basis.

The once-massive Enron Corporation (named America's Most Innovative Company for six years by Fortune magazine and worth $70 billion in its heyday) touted four core values: Respect, Integrity, Communication and Excellence. Shortly after its collapse due to accounting fraud, corruption, and egregious corporate behavior, James Kunen penned an op-ed in the New York Times dissecting those values and questioning what is behind writing vision statements. Kunen wrote tellingly:

I know one writer who, while struggling to draft one of these corporate credos, threw up her hands in despair and observed: "Why not just come right out and say it? 'We will strive to make as much money as we can without going to prison.'"[10]

Just before the infamous financial services firm Lehman Brothers went belly-up, the execs of their asset management arm, Neuberger Berman, suggested that Lehman Brothers' top executives forego their multi-million dollar bonuses to send a unified message to investors and employees that management wasn't shirking their responsibility for being accountable for sub-par performance. Interestingly enough, that idea was laughed at and dismissed with a Lehman executive director saying, "I am not sure what's in the water at Neuberger Berman..." and apologized for whoever suggested such a stupid idea.

On the other hand, way back in 1943 Robert Wood Johnson personally wrote Johnson & Johnson's mission statement as a credo that would guide the company philosophically and behaviorally. But three decades-and-a-half later, CEO James Burke challenged his top execs with this question: do we still believe this? Seriously.

He reminded them bluntly, "If we're not going to live by it, let's tear it off the wall."

The Johnson & Johnson credo listed the responsibilities of their company, first to doctors, nurses, patients, moms and dads who trusted the quality of their products, then secondly to their own employees, promising "competent management" and actions that were "just and ethical."

Next, they listed their responsibility to the communities they lived and worked in as well as the "world community"

---

[10] http://www.nytimes.com/2002/01/19/opinion/enron-s-vision-and-values-thing.html

and cited their social responsibilities—"supporting good works and charities and bearing our fair share of taxes"—along with protecting the environment and resources. Remember, this was in 1943, long before corporate social responsibility became trendy. Last, they acknowledged their responsibility to their stockholders. Last, mind you.

What followed was a spirited discussion with Burke and his team about the role of morality and ethics in the marketplace. It was followed by a reenergized commitment to the credo and its "true north" discernment in corporate decision-making.

A mere three years later, it was discovered that someone had placed cyanide in the capsules of Tylenol resulting in the deaths of seven people in the Chicago metropolitan area. Johnson & Johnson immediately halted Tylenol production, publicly warned consumers and recalled over thirty million bottles from drugstore shelves at a loss of a quarter-billion dollars in today's money, a decision made by management while Burke was actually on a plane unaware of the Tylenol-reported connection.

Their credo guided a major costly corporate decision… even while their CEO was unreachable.

Writing for the Atlantic Monthly, journalist Jerry Useem[11] contrasted Johnson & Johnson actions to the cover-up by the Volkswagen Corporation regarding a software patch that cheated on emissions tests in their diesel cars. Establishing culture is the responsibility of those at the top; perhaps that's reflected in Ferdinand Piëch, the former CEO of Volkswagen, who, in a corruption trial in 2008 referred to the multi-million dollar funds that paid for

---

[11] Jerry Useem, Atlantic Monthly, December 2015; What Was Volkswagen Thinking?

prostitutes as simply "irregularities." As Useem reports, Piëch chided a lawyer for "mispronouncing *Lamborghini*. ('Those who can't afford one should say it properly' were his precise words.)"[12] Piëch also claimed ignorance of a secret multi-million dollar slush fund at Volkswagen to pay off powerful labor representatives.

But Piëch couldn't have been unaware of this principle: arrogance breeds its own culture.

And it's not just the marketplace: the Church has had its share of self-important, overpaid celebrity pastors who have trashed Paul's admonition to his young mentee, Timothy:

> *They think religion is a way to make a fast buck. A devout life does bring wealth, but it's the rich simplicity of being yourself before God. Since we entered the world penniless and will leave it penniless, if we have bread on the table and shoes on our feet, that's enough. But if it's only money these leaders are after, they'll self-destruct in no time.*[13]

Sadly, it's not uncommon to see pastors exposed in the news for some major moral implosion. The seductive trio of money, sex and power affects even those who were considered spiritually bulletproof by their followers. The not-so-subliminal response from the general public is typically centered on integrity: a cynical "I-told-you-so" when a spiritual leader's walk doesn't match their talk.

True integrity-oriented leaders take an integrated, big-picture approach to their organizations. Let's look at each of the points of the *Organizational Integrity Triangle*.

---

[12] ibid.
[13] 1 Timothy 6:5-9 (The Message)

THE ORGANIZATIONAL INTEGRITY TRIANGLE: PERSONAL INTEGRITY

The health and effectiveness of any church and its mission is dependent on the spiritual integrity, vitality, and vision of the leaders—leaders who are healthy, focused and empowered by the Spirit. Healthy, focused churches require healthy, focused leaders because the soul of a local church is bound up

in the heart of its leader or leaders. Whether you're leading a church, organization or ministry, it will invariably look like you.

By personal integrity, I mean the leader's personal wholeness. I can't stress how important this is, even in connection with all the personal requirements of leadership. For instance, in his book *Integrity: The Courage to Meet The Demands of Reality,* Dr. Henry Cloud boils personal leadership down to three qualities…but take notice of Cloud's third critical component:

First, he lists the leader's competency. Cloud notes if you're Bill Gates, "it helps to know something about the computer industry"[14] as Gates obviously did.[15]

---

[14] Dr. Henry Cloud, *Integrity: The Courage to Meet The Demands of Reality* (New York: HarperCollins Publishers; 2006), p.5.

[15] When it comes to competence, one of the best questions leaders can ask themselves is: how am nurturing my leadership abilities? If leadership skills can't be learned, you might as well set this book aside and ascribe to the maxim that "Leaders are born, not made." But consider the research of leadership gurus James Kouzes and Barry Posner. Their data led them to write in their classic book *The Leadership Challenge: How to Make Extraordinary Things Happen in Organizations,* "the theory that there are only a few men and women who can lead us to greatness is just plain wrong. Leadership is a process ordinary people use when they are bringing forth the best from themselves and

The second attribute he stresses is the need for leaders to be able to "build alliances." It's more than just being good at your job; it's the ability to work well with other competent people and create mutually beneficial relationships that make things bigger than what each could accomplish on his or her own. This is where emotional intelligence is crucial.

But as Cloud reminds us, there are millions of people who are bright and can schmooze well. The third critical attribute is: they have to have the character to not screw it up. Too often organizations hire people for their competencies and ultimately fire them for their character. Cloud writes, "Who a person is will ultimately determine if their brains, talents, competencies, energy, effort, deal-making abilities, and opportunities will succeed."[16]

WHO ARE YOU, REALLY?

If integrity is consistency in beliefs, values, and actions, most of us have blind spots in terms of our character. The organizational behavior philosopher Charles Handy made reference to an exercise known as the *Johari Window*, or what he called the *Johari House*. The Johari exercise offers fifty-six character descriptions from which a person chooses six to best describe

others. Leadership is everyone's business." They take a much more inclusive view based on their research and write bluntly: "Liberate the leader in everyone, and extraordinary things happen." The fact that you're reading this book—or any book, article or blog on leadership—means you want to nurture and develop your leadership competencies, to "liberate the leader" in you. You've already started.

[16] ibid. p.8

themselves while their peers are given the same list to choose six, helping to identify the blind spots and hopefully giving the assessee a truer picture of who they are. This picture is then identified with one of the quadrants, or "Rooms."

Room 1 is that part of us that we know about ourselves and others know as well—that's an open person—with a healthy measure of transparency and integrity. Room 2 is the stuff that other people see about us but we are unaware—this is where we have blind spots, where everyone else but us can see our faults or issues. Room 3 is the part of us that we keep private from others—it's our façade, it's how we want others to see us. Room 4 is the place where both we and others are oblivious—it's the unknown.

But Room 4 could more accurately be titled the "God-Only-Knows" quadrant. It is God who can truly reveal to us—or expose if need be—who we really are. He does it in order to bring us true freedom and advance his loving purposes for our lives. It may be a personal revelatory experience between ourselves and God or it may be in the context of a community we're submitted to. This revelation of our true selves becomes more difficult because of the unique insular environment power can create, primarily because leaders often assume they cannot be truly transparent in their communities for fear it will expose a "leadership weakness."

This is where self-leadership must be integrated: we have to be brave enough to take the risk of being vulnerable to allow people to speak into our lives and, in behalf of the organization we lead, in all three points of the integrity triangle.

In the circles I run in, I find most leaders are pretty good at being authentic. I've heard pastors in the tribe I'm a part of say extremely transparent things from the pulpit. But I might add that transparency isn't quite the same as vulnerability. Transparency may be communicating the good and bad about your life for the sake of relate-ability, but vulnerability is allowing trusted people to speak, advise or even rebuke you, to speak *into* your life. Some pastors use the pulpit almost as cathartic therapy, but never actually let people speak into their lives. It's a controlled authenticity: "I have the microphone. You don't."

There's an obvious spiritual principle at work here: vulnerability is simply humility expressed. Being humble is not a doormat attitude or a "nothing-more-than-a-worm" view of oneself, but rather a lack of fear about being known with an ultimate goal of a matured self-forgetfulness.

Best-selling authors and leadership consultants John Gerzema and Michael D'Antonio write tellingly:

> ...Past failure is essential to success. This idea has become so mainstream that those who haven't failed are looked upon skeptically. In our surveys, 86 percent of people believe that having some personal failures is critical to one's overall success. Openness and humility are portals to new relationships and new opportunities and ways of seeing the world. Likewise, your recognizing and engaging with the vulnerabilities of employees makes them more trusting and open. *Vulnerability is the most important agent of change management.* [17] (italics mine).

Gerzema and D'Antonio offered a chilling statistic at the time of their writing:

> Cisco Systems estimates that by 2020, fifty billion devices will transmit data to the Internet, creating a stream of information that can be tapped by consumers, business

---

[17] John Gerzema, Michael D'Antonio, *The Athena Doctrine: How Men (And Women Who Think Like Them) Will Rule the Future* (San Francisco, Jossey-Bass, 2013), p.263

competitors, public officials and the press. In this age of connectivity, masculine-style hidden backroom dealings will inevitably fall prey to highly observant sensors that will force things out into the open. In this "glass house" environment, organizations must be as open as possible, keepings its dealings honest and above board."[18]

Regardless of your politics, Wikileaks introduced us to a secular version of a future world not too unlike Jesus' description of the Kingdom of God:

> *"The time is coming when everything that is covered up will be revealed, and all that is secret will be made known to all. Whatever you have said in the dark will be heard in the light, and what you have whispered behind closed doors will be shouted from the housetops for all to hear!"* [19]

Ouch.

Leaders of the future will be free from the need to be seen as bulletproof, independent and all-knowing. A "soft-skills" leadership approach is also the best antidote for a pervasive cynical culture and the ability to function in our new über-interdependent world.

I have seen too many leaders with strong leadership gifts fall apart because of character issues or lack of self-awareness. Some were spiritually mature but emotionally under-developed, others were emotionally mature and spiritually under-developed. How many leaders were in the news over the last few years because of character failure? Every leader has to be diligent at this. It breaks my heart to hear of a church leader with so much potential do something that shatters his or her integrity, and thus affects the bigger picture. We have to cultivate a healthy measure of self-

---

[18] ibid p.261
[19] Luke 12:2, 3 (New Living Translation)

awareness, which means we have to have some permission-giving systems built into our lives.

Do we have people in our lives that we give permission to speak truth to us—to rebuke, to correct, to probe—without fear of retribution? Do we ask them periodically: what do you see in me that's frustrating to you? How am I doing as a leader…as a friend?

And then do I also do that at a divine level as well? Have I given Jesus permission to reveal areas of my life where integrity is questioned? Do I schedule "searchlight" times with Jesus? That's why David wrote a song to God that expressed, *Search me, O God, and know my heart; test me and know my anxious thoughts. See if there is any offensive way in me, and lead me in the way everlasting.*[20]

Seriously consider these questions as a leader: How vulnerable am I? How willing am I to be corrected? How open to the voice of the Holy Spirit am I for a reprimand? As a follower of Jesus, if I'm not periodically hearing the whispers of the Spirit saying, "Don't allow your thoughts to wander there"…"Forgive him"…"Don't defend yourself on this one," then I need to question the depth of my relationship with God.

Self-leadership means that we notch up our level of self-awareness, and that usually means finding places where we are willing to take the risk of being vulnerable—because a blind spot is just that: a blind spot. And if we really want to help others grow as whole people, then we need to discover our own stuff.

This aspect of self-awareness is why Jesus asked,

> "Why worry about a speck in your friend's eye when you have a log in your own? How can you think of saying, 'Friend,

---

[20] Psalm 139:23-24

let me help you get rid of that speck in your eye,' when you can't see past the log in your own eye? Hypocrite! First get rid of the log from your own eye; then perhaps you will see well enough to deal with the speck in your friend's eye."[21]

Or as the airline attendant says prior to takeoff, "Place your own oxygen mask on first before you assist others."

What might happen in our churches, nonprofits, companies and families if leaders became more transparent with the failures of their organizations...and their own?

THE ORGANIZATIONAL INTEGRITY TRIANGLE: MISSIONAL INTEGRITY

The second component on the *Organizational Integrity Triangle* is *Missional* integrity. There is a plethora of books about mission and vision, so I'll not flog a dead horse here. Sometimes those words are used interchangeably, but for simplicity sake, I define vision as "what you want  your organization to be when it grows up." A preferred future. Mission is what you want your organization to do. Or in the Kingdom of God, it's what you believe the Holy Spirit has called you to be...and what you are called to do.

Let's personalize this. One thing that identifies people who are healthy and productive spiritually and emotionally is their measure of self-awareness. Self-awareness is seeing yourself as you really are in order that God can work into you what he sees as your potential. What we keep or hide from God is what hinders our spiritual and emotional

---

[21] Luke 6:41-42 (New Living Translation)

growth. Self-awareness is ultimately about searching and finding the answer to two big philosophical questions in life: who am I and why am I here?

But just like people, organizations as diverse as corporations to churches often have little self-awareness. Why does the organization exist? Strategic church leaders must come to a place where they wrestle with those same questions for their church. They take their people through difficult times and changes to fulfill their purpose as an organization. Wrestling with those questions will lead you to discover what your mission is. We *do* out of who we *are*.

Are you really clear on what your church, your ministry, is to be focused on? The mission I spent a third of my life on was: To love the people of Cincinnati into relationship with Jesus and give away to the world what God has given us. I could say that in my sleep. Years ago in a church survey, we offered a multiple-choice question with five great church mission statements. Ninety-five percent of our people identified our mission correctly. That was a win.

It had taken our leadership team months of discussion and debate to develop and wordsmith a finalized mission and vision statement. We knew that our mission statement had to reflect what we had been called to do, the divine vocation for our church. We had the nutshell of our mission statement for years previously and had done our best to hear God through each other, through our history, and through the Spirit.

But our vision was a creative picture, a metaphor, of what we wanted to look like and who we wanted to be. It also had to include some statement of how we would primarily accomplish this. We finished our vision picture with a section called, "We will be—." In the end, it read like this:

VINEYARD COMMUNITY CHURCH

The Mission
To love the people of Cincinnati into relationship with Jesus Christ and give away to the world what God has given us.

The Vision
Imagine a ragtag collection of surrendered and transformed people who love God and others. They are mesmerized by the idea that this is not about them, but all about Jesus. They are transfixed by his story and his heart for their city. They are seedthrowers and firestarters, hope peddlers and grace-givers, risktakers and dreamers, young and old. They link arms with anyone who tells the story of Jesus. They empower the poor, strengthen the weak, embrace the outcast, seek the lost. They serve together, play together, worship together, live life together. Their city will change because God sent them.
They are us.
We believe that small things done with great love will change the world.

We Will Be
A diverse, celebratory church of missional, disciple-making communities in every neighborhood.
A relational citywide network strategized on reaching Greater Cincinnati.
Reproducers and developers of outward-focused churches worldwide.

Not only would we teach through this statement periodically on the weekends and incorporate the phrases in our orientation and training sessions, we typically would have this looping on our video screens before and after each service. It was our hope that the language would permeate the collective consciousness of our people, that they would refer to themselves as firestarters or hope peddlers or grace-givers and desire to live lives that were outward-focused and self-forgetful.

But there's a catch: the present love affair with corporate mission statements must be more than a framed eight-by-twelve well-wordsmithed paragraph hung on a wall. It's one thing to have a clear focus...and another thing to actually do it.

I walked into a fast-food chain restaurant a while back that was a hot mess; bad leadership breeds bad service, bad attitudes, and bad atmosphere. Next to the cash register where you placed your order, was a framed mission statement, something about "friendly service," "quality food," "fun," and so on.

But behind the cash register was a smirking teenager who wanted to be anywhere else on the planet but there. And I don't blame him: the bathroom hadn't been cleaned in months. The laminated tables were sticky. The windowsills were graveyards for flies. I'm pretty sure one of the two glass entrance doors had never been unlatched since opening day. The mission statement wasn't worth the plastic frame it was screwed to the wall in.

What good is a mission statement that's never referenced? At what point will the manager have a wake-up call for missional integrity?

Wrestling with missional integrity will force even deeper work. For instance, at Vineyard Cincinnati we knew that the only way to exponentially accomplish our defined mission was ultimately by building *outward-focused* disciples. But we even had to redefine for our people what a disciple was... otherwise, they would put their own language on it and it may not have reflected our DNA.

And so over and over we would remind people at Vineyard Cincinnati that a *disciple is a surrendered and transformed person who loves God and others.* That's as simple as it gets. But that forced us to get fiercely honest: were we actually creating that?

If I lead a church of fifteen people that's been the same size for fifteen years and I say my mission is to turn people who don't yet know Jesus into passionate servants of Christ, I'm overdue for a moment of truth telling. And if I'm sending someone out of that fifteen people to plant a church because I think that church-planting is one of the most effective forms of evangelism, then again I need to be honest: the chances are pretty good that the new church-plant will have the same DNA and will largely be ineffective if its mission is primarily one of evangelism.

I'm not trying to suggest what your mission should be and I'm not talking about the size of our churches, but I am saying we must be honest as it relates to *what we say our mission is.* And guaranteed, your mission and vision is what will keep your heart pumping as a leader and will be the primary catalyst for how people will respond to you: people respond to vision far more than to needs.

THE ORGANIZATIONAL INTEGRITY TRIANGLE: SYSTEMIC INTEGRITY

In 1999, NASA lost a $125 million spacecraft because engineers failed to convert U.S. standards to metric. The navigation team in one lab used one standard while the engineers who designed and built it in a different company used the other…and no one caught the miss until the Mars probe disappeared behind the red planet at an altitude that was way too low and never regained contact. No one caught the mistake for the entire nine months the probe took to make the over four-hundred-million-mile journey.

"People sometimes make errors," said Dr. Damon Weiler, NASA's Associate Administrator for Space Science. "The problem here was not the error, it was the failure of NASA's systems engineering, and the checks and balances in our processes to detect the error. That's why we lost the spacecraft."[22]

John Logsdon, director of George Washington University's space policy institute, was a bit more direct. "That is so dumb," he said. "There seems to have emerged over the past couple of years a systematic problem in the space community of insufficient attention to detail."[23]

It had been a bad number of years for the space agency; some blamed cost-cutting measures, bad quality control, and poor management. One thing was sure: there was a systems breakdown.

And that brings us to the last point on the *Organizational Integrity Triangle: Systemic* integrity. Do you have the systems and processes in place to support your mission? Are resources being put toward the things that drive the mission? Is the organiza-

tion built to support the mission? Are the right people in the right seats? Do you have the right volunteer leaders in every area? Are you providing enough structure for them so the mission can be accomplished? Are you resourcing them for

---

[22] http://mars.jpl.nasa.gov/msp98/news/mco990930.html
[23] http://articles.latimes.com/1999/oct/01/news/mn-17288

what they need to accomplish the mission? Do they know if they are achieving success? Do they have clear goals? Do they feel supported?

Leaders have to pay close attention to organizational systems, no matter how unsexy the work may seem.

Everything you do is dependent on a system. Consider how the human body is designed and the intricate interdependency and interplay of disparate organs and chemistry: we even refer to our nervous *system*...or our respiratory *system*...or digestive *system*. Every organism and organization function via some sort of system. There's a reason we go to the doctor periodically for a physical—we're actually doing a systems analysis. Why would we not do that with the organization we've been entrusted with? Periodically, an honest audit of our systems, goals, and strategies is vital, whether it's done internally or by an outside group.

This little dust ball of a planet is spinning within a solar *system*. I live within a specific family *system*. I'm writing on a notebook computer with a particular operating *system*. If there was not a process for the different elements to function, we would be in trouble.

I have to smile when people tell me that they are spiritual, but they don't believe in organized religion. What's the alternative—disorganized religion? We must have systems to bring structure to our relationships, to apply gifts and skills appropriately, unify our values, and accomplish our corporate purpose.

Suppose you say that your mission is to create an awesome worship experience for believers each weekend, and you've got a sound system from three decades ago and a keyboard from Big Lots, then I have doubts that you're really organized to resource your mission. If half the worship team doesn't show up each week, something is breaking down in the system.

Developing healthy systems requires forethought, strategy, and planning. It's becoming much rarer in churches today, but I can remember in certain schools-of-thought that strategic planning was seen as being anti-Holy Spirit—as if we were boxing in the Spirit of God. Those of us who came from more charismatic backgrounds loved these verses in James: *Now listen, you who say, "Today or tomorrow we will go to this or that city, spend a year there, carry on business and make money." Why, you do not even know what will happen tomorrow.*[24]

But somehow we overlooked the plethora of Biblical passages on planning...and particularly the unique ways that Jesus planned his ministry.

For instance, Jesus had short-term plans and goals, as expressed when some Pharisees came and told him that Herod was coming to kill him. In a tough-as-nails response, Jesus said, *"Tell that fox that I've no time for him right now. Today and tomorrow I'm busy clearing out the demons and healing the sick; the third day I'm wrapping things up."*[25]

His Three-Year-Plan was Luke 4:18-19. *"The Spirit of the Lord is upon me. He has anointed me to preach good news to the poor. He has sent me to proclaim freedom to the prisoners and recovery of sight to the blind, to release the oppressed, to announce the time of God's favor."* He seemed to know that this was a multi-year plan of modeling a clear mission and even told people in the early stages of his ministry not to tell anyone who healed them.

---

[24] James 4:13, 14
[25] Luke 13:32 (The Message Version)

Finally, Jesus had a Several-Thousand-Year Plan: The Church. *"On this rock I will build my church and the gates of hell won't prevail..."*[26]

Jesus had a system by which he would accomplish his objective of building a collection of people through whom he would roll out the Kingdom of God, his rule and reign.

What is your system for accomplishing your mission? Do you have a system by which your personal integrity is nurtured and held accountable? All three points on the *Organizational Integrity Triangle* are interrelated and interdependent.

STRATEGIC PLANNING: AN EXAMPLE

Part of our system for strategic planning was annually determining what our primary initiatives would be for the upcoming year. We would typically want to focus our entire staff and key volunteer leaders on three-to-five initiatives or objectives. My overall performance as senior pastor would be reflected in how well we as a church accomplished these initiatives by the end of the year.

Our system would often incorporate these steps: first, we would hold an initial meeting with our shareholders[27] (our members) that would be centered on a prayer exercise to help them hear from God what he wanted us to focus on.

---

[26] Matthew 16:18b

[27] Our shareholder numbers typically reflected a version of Pareto's Law: 20% of our weekend attendance would identify themselves as shareholders, covenanting with the church to be in a small group, give percentage-wise to Vineyard Cincinnati, regularly serve in an outward-focused manner, and other somewhat arbitrary sacrifices that reflected our core values.

This would typically be twenty-minute individual "alone time"-guided prayer in print with questions, then gathered into groups to share what they heard with "scribes" assigned for each group. Later, that info would be collated and categorized into themes and passed on to the elder team

Next, the elder team (a combination of trustees and staff executive leadership team) would meet and share their own thoughts and observations after looking over the shareholders' responses.

After that, the staff executive team would take a two-day retreat for prayer and to develop and initially wordsmith the strategic initiatives, with the finished version to be approved by the trustees.

During that two-day retreat, the staff executive team would also sketch out a rough teaching calendar for the next year—series themes would be mapped on a calendar. We would keep five things in focus during this process:

+ Our mission and vision (it would be posted on a wall)
+ Our core values (posted as well)
+ Our proposed new strategic initiatives
+ A gap analysis (where is there a problem of praxis at Vineyard Cincinnati? What are the felt needs?)
+ And, of course, what is God saying? (a guided prayer time)

We would also balance and adjust our teaching calendar through this filter: "Army" talks (series that are mission-centered, "take-the-hill" focused), "School" talks (series that are doctrinal, creedal, or pure Biblical-literacy messages) and "Hospital" talks (growth-and-healing, soul care, self-awareness series).

Too much of one style can either respectively wear a church out, "puff" it up, or lead it to become too inward-focused.

Eventually, the finished strategic initiatives and teaching calendar were then presented to the whole staff. Next, ministry directors and their teams would begin the process of creating their own ministry plans and budgets, based as much as possible, on the new strategic initiatives. Directors would then present their ministry plans and budgets to the executive leadership team and then all plans and budgets would be fully developed and approved by the trustees.

The entire process with all its checks and balances would take approximately six to seven months but would thoroughly guide our focus for the following year.

THE POWER OF SYSTEMS

When it comes to systems, think of the difference between George Whitefield and John Wesley, both dynamic preachers during the Great Awakening of the mid-1700's that radically shook England and the colonies. Whitefield became one of the greatest orators, a veritable rock star of his generation. Benjamin Franklin—himself not a confessing Christian—described the effects of Whitefield's preaching on the colonists in his autobiography:

> It was wonderful to see the Change soon made in the Manners [behavior] of our Inhabitants; from being thoughtless or indifferent about Religion, it seem'd as if all the World were growing Religious; so that one could not walk thro' the Town in an Evening without Hearing Psalms sung in different Families of every Street. [28]

Then Franklin described the sheer power of Whitefield's voice:

---

[28] http://nationalhumanitiescenter.org/pds/becomingamer/ideas/text2/franklin whitefield.pdf

He had a loud and clear Voice, and articulated his Words and Sentences so perfectly that he might be heard and understood at a great Distance . . . I computed that he might well be heard by more than Thirty Thousand. This reconcil'd me to the Newspaper Accounts of his having preach'd to 25,000 People in the Fields. [29]

This was two hundred years before subwoofers. Pretty impressive. God powerfully used Whitefield.

But John Wesley developed a system, a *method* (hence, Methodists) for developing disciples in a small group system that could be reproduced. Wesley believed the effectiveness of the revival waned because converts had no spiritual accountability, comparing their lack of training and support to "begetting children for the murderer."[30]

Wesley created a sustaining multi-generational system whose long-term effectiveness arguably outstripped Whitefield's conversions, as impressive as they were.

Systems don't have to be complicated (and less so in smaller organizations), but they do have to be clear about the process they are designed to accomplish. No matter how large a church is, questions like these—and this is not a comprehensive list—must be answered:

1. *How do people who are far from God find him through us?* (evangelism)

2. *How do we corporately and intimately connect with God?* (worship)

3. *How do we help new people integrate into the life of the church?* (assimilation)

4. *How do we help people grow into the likeness of Christ?* (discipleship)

---

[29] ibid.
[30] John Wesley; Journals; August 25, 1763, p.169

5. *How do we help people form safe and growing communities?* (small groups)

6. *How are we recruiting/training/releasing leaders?* (leadership development)

7. *How do we think about and plan together our goals and our future?* (strategic planning)

8. *How are we led as a church?* (leadership/governance)

9. *How do we tell each other what we're doing, where we're going and why?* (communication)

These are all systems questions. The answers won't be the same for everyone, but they have to be thought through.

A WHOLE CHURCH MODEL

Let me offer a simple tool for assessing any fractures in the integrity of your church systems with this "Body of Christ" model developed by my friend Garry Shirk. It represents the process by which the Body of Christ— the Church—now functions like Jesus in the scope of how we connect people with the Kingdom of God. Jesus modeled the *Body of Christ* ministry over three years, with lots of crowds and with a smaller number of followers, twelve disciples, and three insiders.

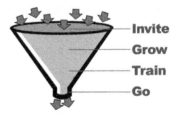

BODY OF CHRIST MODEL

Invite
Grow
Train
Go

We begin with *Invite. Invite* is simply whatever method you use to introduce people to Jesus and his kingdom. There were times when Jesus attracted huge crowds, as when he taught from a boat because of the crowd along the lakeshore, or when he walked up the mountain to speak after "seeing the multitudes" that were gathering. He traveled town-to-town, garnering crowds that were attracted to his authoritative speaking, his unique welfare program (two fish and five loaves!) and the power encounters and healings taking place. His colorful stories and cultural head-tilting analogies filled crowds with wonder. The question here is simply: *what are we doing to find and/or attract people who are far away from God?*

He taught as well in synagogues and smaller settings (dinner parties, weddings, etcetera), again offering parables and poking at the religious establishment. In these smaller settings, we have the ability to grow people spiritually and emotionally by digging deeper into spiritual truths and offering practical applications as a result of those truths. The invitational component is now seesawing with challenge. This is the *Grow* stage in the model and the place where we simply ask ourselves: *what helps people grow?*

In the *Train* stage, there is a subset of people who get more attention, more "hands-on" preparation and development for leadership. It's more Socratic and equipping, with a clear expectation that one would be doing similar work that Jesus did. When Jesus sent the seventy-two out on the first mission trip, there were specific instructions (after obvious modeling from Jesus) and reinforcing feedback when they returned for debriefing. In this stage, there's a clear end in mind for the people we're training...and the obvious question here is: *how are they trained for mission?*

But with the eleven, even clearer authority and power was eventually imparted...and the loop was completed: they would now take on the role of Jesus as not only healers and communicators of the Kingdom, but disciplers who would invite, grow and train others as Jesus taught them.[31] This is the *Go* stage where people are empowered with real authority and launched into spiritual leadership at some level.

At each one of these stages we have to be honest with ourselves as leaders and question how we're doing at each juncture. I can't tell you what your system or methodology should be for each one of those stages—it's more than likely unique to your culture and demographic—but I am suggesting that if all four categories are not functioning in a healthy way, your ministry or church is heading for extinction.

STAGES OF ORGANIZATIONAL FOCUS

Thinking hard about systems is a critical component for organizational integrity. But one caveat: if you're in the front end of churchplanting or leading a fairly new and small church, it's never too early to be thinking about systems, but it shouldn't be your primary focus. After all, you're mostly centered on gathering and sheer survival and your systemic needs are much simpler at this point. But just like people, your churchplant will go through changes in focus as well. The typical foci of a church tend to look like this:

Stages of Organizational Focus

| Personality focus | Mission focus | Systems focus | Franchise focus |

When a church is first planted, it's primarily personality-centered; it's all about the churchplanter—their ability to gather, the force of their personality, the sense of this-is-a-person-I-want-to-follow, and so forth. It means lots of

---

lunch, breakfast and dinner meetings with potential followers who are probing the leader's competency, calling and character.

Next, the church must move toward becoming *mission-centered*. This is critical: it has to grow beyond the planter's personality and the mission must become bigger than him or her. Don't get attendance necessarily mixed up with this—it's not numbers-oriented; there are huge churches that are personality-centered and in deep danger...as well as small personality-cult churches.

As the church or organization gets more complex and multilayered, systems and processes become even more critical. Considerable effort must be made to ensure effective communication, productivity (or fruitfulness in Biblical terms), and departmental interdependency and engagement.

The last stage is *franchising*. For a church, this could mean launching a new churchplant, a satellite, an entrepreneurial ministry, a non-profit, a food pantry, or whatever. At this point, an organization has had enough experience to launch more holistic and reproducible endeavors. It's necessary to launch new enterprises or even hive off for organizational health.

REFLECTION POINTS

Take some time to meditate and mull over questions like these:

+ How grounded is your organization? Be honest. The Earth element represents the foundational health of both you as a leader, the team that you lead and your organization. It is in the earth that trees root, find their nutrition and spread their leaves to catch the sun's life-sustaining energy.

+ If you're a pastor, is there a deep undercurrent of rooted wholeness in your church…and in you?

+ Are you driven by your values and principles…and are your values and principles rooted in God's heart for people?

+ Do you find yourself spending more time putting out fires rather than building values and a missional sensibility into people?

Elemental leaders understand how critical and foundational this essential element is. But as important as it is, our next chapter unpacks the power of passion: what it is and what it isn't…and how this vital fire fuels every organization.

CHAPTER 3
FIRE | PASSION

"There was once a day when we asked prospective staff about academic accomplishment. Today, the number one question is 'What is your passion in ministry?' *It's hard to overstate the need for passion.*"

~LYLE SCHALLER

"Enthusiasm is one of the most powerful engines of success. When you do a thing, do it with all your might. Put your whole soul into it. Stamp it with your own personality. Be active, be energetic and faithful, and you will accomplish your object. *Nothing great was ever achieved without enthusiasm."*

~RALPH WALDO EMERSON

And whatever you do, *do it heartily,*
as to the Lord and not to men…

~PAUL, THE APOSTLE

've been on both sides of transitioning a lead pastor. Years before serving in the lead pastor role at our church, everyone on staff—including me—shared our individual scores from a leadership assessment we had each completed. It turned out that one of the labels for a specific style of leadership was termed "dominant." This stereotypically tended to be the hard-charging, no-holds-barred, take-the-hill leaders. The primary leaders in our organization seemed to fit that mold. I was okay with that; after all, it was hard to argue with success. After we compared test results, all the strong "D" personalities were high-fiving each other and comparing notes, mostly because they happened to be the same leadership type as my friend and lead pastor.

It made sense to me: we were a mission-driven church and fairly intoxicated with our annual up-and-to-the-right charts, rapid growth, and adrenalin addiction. We would eventually be adding an identical seventh weekend celebration in a room that only seated five-hundred-and-seventy.

But I remember thinking, "I'll never be a real leader here. I don't have that kind of personality-type." My predominant style happened to be "inspirational," which seemed to me like the softer side of leadership. Okay, maybe even the weaker side of leadership. Who wants to be led by a Hallmark card?—as I misunderstood it.

I don't remember feeling particularly sad about that; it was simply a reality-check. I enjoyed what I was doing then. I led worship, taught a midweek Bible study, and had launched a Saturday night celebration for singles that had morphed into a regular weekend service. I taught on the weekends periodically. I developed creative teams and led several ministry areas as well as facilitated multiple small groups. Sometimes I spoke in workshops and seminars in our tribe.

But I was not a "jump-in-front, take-charge" leader. I didn't swim with the sharks; I dog-paddled with dolphins. I didn't care to know Attila's secrets; the rules of war weren't on my radar. Anything that smelled manipulative creeped me out. I valued harmony, while conflict totally sucked the energy out of me. And I frankly didn't care about position, posturing or the politics of power. Boring.

My real problem was this: my paradigm of leadership was way too small. And limited.

Situational leadership was new to me, let alone understanding the seasons and sovereignty of God. But even more was a past that dogged me. Inferiority floated like pond scum across my gene pool. Plus, a few good failures rounded out my life-experiences.

Regardless of the reasons, one thing was true: I was a classic reluctant leader. I didn't view myself with blue face-paint leading a charge on horseback. Nor was I the gladiator Maximus charging the chariots in a coliseum.

I would have lived in the suburbs of Sparta.

The Bible is filled with a wide spectrum of leaders. Moses was a seriously reluctant leader after his first big failure in life. Caleb was an aggressively confident one. Gideon begged to get off the leadership hook. David said simply, "I've killed both a lion and a bear with my hands. Let's go after this uncircumcised Philistine," and the Bible records that he ran *toward* Goliath. The apostle Paul seemed to be a "my-way-or-the-highway" leader early on. Timothy was timid. Each of them had different pasts, different life experiences, but they were all leaders with decidedly different approaches to leadership. The danger is that we can overlook a potential leader for the one with the dominant take-charge personality.

The truth is: everyone follows someone and everyone leads someone. For instance, we are invited, no, demanded by Jesus, to disciple and mentor others. No one is excused. The scope of our leadership will differ widely based on what we've been given; to whom much is given, much is required, but it's explicit in scriptures that everyone is called to lead and help others to develop a relationship with God.[32]

But there is no leadership without fire, without a passion that will drive even the reluctant leader to step forward...to do the right thing.

My problem was compounded by a misunderstanding of passion: what it was and wasn't.

WHAT PASSION IS...AND ISN'T

Shortly after I surrendered my life to God, I read of a Christian music festival in the hills of Pennsylvania, nearly ten hours away. I was twenty-one years old, threw a sleeping bag into my AMC Gremlin (don't judge me...) and took off, arriving in the middle of the night to set up a pup tent in a rainstorm. In the morning, I walked over a hill to discover twenty-some-thousand young people gathering in a valley. Jesus freaks. I didn't know there were that many Christians in the whole world. We were in the throes of the Jesus Movement.

These were ex-druggies, ex-hippies, musicians, and youth groups all thrown together. An animated young man took the stage and did something I had never heard: a Jesus cheer. He shouted, "Give me a 'J'!"

---

[32] Matthew 28:18-20

In the drug world, I knew that meant something else. The crowd shouted back "'J'!"

"Give me an 'E'!" And then he went through the whole name.

It was very weird. Was that the way Christians were supposed to act? Like cheerleaders? Back then, that sounded more like a high school pep rally to me. Was that passion? Was that how I was supposed to respond if I was passionate about Jesus? Though I wasn't sure of that particular expression, I knew I was hungry for God.

Even though it's been highjacked by our sex-saturated culture, the word passion comes to us from Latin meaning "to suffer"…as in the passion of the Christ. It means that you can feel so deeply about something or someone that it costs you and hurts.

Louis Psihoyos is a documentary filmmaker who won an Academy Award for his film *The Cove*, an exposé on the brutal slaughter of dolphins in a Japanese fishing town and the subsequent health concerns due to mercury content from the meat. Years later *Wired* magazine interviewed him on a current project he was working on at that time called *Racing Extinction* in which he met with scientists who reported that the planet was experiencing species extinctions "1,000 times faster than the natural rate."[33]

Psihoyos is a passionate filmmaker on a mission. He has literally risked his life to film in locations that would be extremely hostile if discovered.

Why would someone do that?

In his interview with reporter Andy Isaacson, Psihoyos revealed a personal story from thirty years earlier that haunted him to this day. He described walking around a

---

[33] Andy Isaacson; Wired magazine; "Attention Humanity!"; September 2015

busy flea market outside of Philadelphia, strolling behind a mother and father with their two children. It was a beautiful day—music playing, crowds laughing—when suddenly a pickup truck pulled up behind the family. From his angle he could tell the big side mirrors on it might hit the family. He yelled out but instantly noticed people looking uncomfortably at him; after all, who screams in public? He started to shout out again but held back because of feeling self-conscious.

In that brief moment of hesitation, the truck's mirror struck the two children, knocking them under the wheels of the truck.

"They died right in front of me,' Psihoyos says. His lips are quivering. "…and I realized that it was my weakness. This family was crushed; two lives were extinguished. And it was because I was too f—g embarrassed to scream in a crowd."

Psihoyos brushes a tear with his finger, becoming more impassioned. "Now, if you believe that we're losing half the species on the planet and it's because of our *behavior?* If we're burning oil because *it's cheap?* We're losing this world before we have a chance to understand that it's here. I think about that family that died because I couldn't speak up, and now I look at my whole world dying. Everything that we've known. I don't mind being the guy screaming in the room at this point. If I can tell it in a beautiful, elegant way and take people on an interesting ride, I'll scream as loud as I can."[34]

Regardless of how one feels about Psihoyos filmmaking tactics or worldview, one can only admire his reflective transparency regarding a painful regret at a flea market thirty

---

[34] ibid.

years prior…and his now impassioned efforts to shout to the world his critical environmental message.

He is passionate.

Passion is marked by a willingness to do anything, or as Saint Bernard of Clairvaux expressed, *"The true measure of loving God is to love him without measure."*

God has called us to love him with all our heart, soul, strength and mind. But he doesn't stop there: we're called to do likewise with our neighbor, the people around us. He demands an internal drive that compels us to think missionally.

Instead, in our churches we often hear more about self-control and what we're *not* supposed to do…instead of a passionate craving, a hunger, for God and the people he loves. Or as C. S. Lewis put it:

> It would seem that Our Lord finds our desires not too strong, but too weak. We are half-hearted creatures, fooling about with drink and sex and ambition when infinite joy is offered us, like an ignorant child who wants to go on making mud pies in a slum because he cannot imagine what is meant by the offer of a holiday at the sea. We are far too easily pleased.[35]

Consider brand-new parents you've bumped into at the store; before you can say congratulations, they've already scrolled a dozen photos of their newborn for you on their smartphones. They're posting pictures minute-by-minute of their golden child's activities. Personally, I love watching parents offer pictures of their kids and talk about them. I have a favorite picture that my wife took of our two girls when they were toddlers, but even now as adults, I love to

---

[35] C.S. Lewis; *The Weight of Glory, and Other Addresses* (New York, HarperCollins, 1980), p.27

talk about them and describe their personalities and the things that make them special in my eyes.

Have you ever wondered how God would describe his kids, what the model son or daughter would look like? Can you imagine God pulling out his cosmic wallet and yanking a picture out? We actually have an account of him doing that. When Jesus was baptized by John, God effuses, "That's my boy...and am I ever proud of him!"

That's passion.

Everyone needs someone or something to fight for, something to give your life to, something to die for. That's why a self-focused life is so unfulfilling, why it never satisfies even the best narcissist. Think about it: you cannot die for yourself. It makes sense that Jesus said the greatest expression of love is when someone gives his life for another. If I don't have anything to die for, then I really don't have anything for which to live. In other words, if what I'm living for right now isn't worth dying for, I'm already dead. Or as the screenwriter Randall Wallace put in the mouth of William Wallace in *Braveheart*, "All men die. Not all men really live."

Have you identified what you're truly passionate about? We can actually know by asking ourselves, "For what would I give my life?" Passion is extravagant. It doesn't consider the cost.

THE EXTRAVAGANCE OF PASSION

In the New Testament, Luke records an account of extravagant passion. One night, a well-known local religious leader throws a big dinner party and invites Jesus. During the dinner, the town prostitute slinks into the room behind Jesus. Suddenly, she begins to sob uncontrollably and falls wordlessly on the feet of Jesus, drenching them with her tears. Unceremoniously, she lets her hair down, slowly dries his feet with it and kisses them. Then, in that electrified hushed room, she pulls out an alabaster bottle of ridiculously expensive perfume, perhaps the most valuable thing she owns, and pours it on his feet.[36]

Imagine the supercharged atmosphere of the room in this moment. Think of the risk a prostitute took in a patriarchal religious culture to barge into a roomful of men and pour out her most precious treasure on the dusty feet of an itinerant preacher from a backwoods town in Galilee. To the controlled and dispassionate person, this seems fanatical, uncomfortable and over-the-top wasteful.

Passion is focused on the object and the outcome, the end result. Jesus came resolutely to die for our sins. He began with the end in mind and was passionate about accomplishing it. We know that from the beginning of his ministry that he knew his final destination would be Jerusalem. Passion is focused on a desired outcome. The Bible says he suffered through the shame and agony of the cross for the joy set before him.[37] That's because of passion.

Likewise with organizations…and the mission for which they exist. Passionate organizations will always begin with the leader. People are neither attracted to or will ultimately follow a leader that isn't pursuing an oversized, compelling dream.

And you can't fake true passion. We can see through the used-car huckster. Or the sobbing televangelist who promises prosperity in exchange for a love-gift. Or the fawning

---

[36] Luke 7:37-38 (The Message Version)
[37] Hebrews 12:2a

phony who flatters you. One simply "can't fool all the people all the time." Eventually, pseudo-passion is exposed.

At one point in my leadership at the church, we were internally going through some difficult times. For various reasons there was disunity between myself and the board, I had personally been pulled into a lawsuit that had no merit (it eventually made its way to the Ohio Supreme Court and was tossed out), we had only a few years earlier gone through an entire restructuring of our governance model, and, to make matters worse, had flatlined in our growth, which created a strain in our finances with our new facility. After hiring a high-powered "change agent" in our leadership structure, we experienced a thirty-percent staff turnover in a single year. The ripples of those departures, however justified they may have been, created a simmering unease in our church.

The problems had become the center of all my conversations at home and seemed all-consuming. I felt like a complete failure and found myself in a depression.

One day I was having lunch with my friend Dwight Wilkens, the pastor of an African-American church not far from ours. We had been in a small group together for several years. Dwight was a big dude; he came out of the projects to play football at Ohio State University during the Woody Hayes era, even going to the Rose Bowl back in the day. Years later, he would surrender his life to Jesus.

With his tell-it-like-it-is personality, Dwight suddenly stared hard at me across the restaurant table. "Do you like what you're doing?" he point-blank asked.

I smiled and mumbled a semi-enthusiastic, "Yeah."

There was a long pause. I finally asked, "Why? How come you asked?"

He just looked at me and said, "It just doesn't seem like you do. I don't see a lot of passion." I responded with some lame excuse, but he was absolutely right. I felt dead inside.

A few days later I had a quiet and meek woman in the church tell me that she had been praying for me and sensed God prompting her to tell me, "Don't let the skirmishes cause you to miss the war." I had not chosen my battles carefully and had allowed the problems to steal the deep, abiding joy that God promises his followers. What's more, it had robbed me of my passion for the top-line mission of the Kingdom of God and his heart for people.

Without passion, I was dead in the water. It took another year for me to recover. I have no other words to describe it, but God visited my brokenness with a radical outpouring of his Spirit and reaffirmed my calling: a "leadership switch" was flipped on in my heart. A year later we launched our biggest initiative ever with a renewed vigor and church-wide excitement. At the risk of sounding leader-centric, the very energy of the church was affected by my passion-depression.

Spiritual leaders must foster genuine passion if they want passionate organizations. It starts with you: what stokes excitement and dedication in you for God and his mission? Nurturing and developing passion at a personal level is another book altogether, but you probably intuitively know what your spiritual pathways are; I would certainly recommend the writings of Dallas Willard or Gary Thomas. For me, taking the time to worship God via music, reading apologetics that challenge me intellectually, or simply asking trusted, passionate people to lay hands on me and pray, can each increase my awe of God.

Yet it's one thing to be passionate about God and his mission and another to be able to infect others with a corporate expression of it and to create what Ken Blanchard famously called "raving fans." So the obvious question is: what stirs passion in others and focuses them toward a common vision? If elemental leaders provide catalytic heat to situations, what fuels organizational passion best?

I've observed six primary firestarters for any organization; the first three are linear in progression, the last three each stand alone as potentially creating corporate cohesive movement and effectiveness.

FIRESTARTER #1: DISSATISFACTION WITH THE STATUS QUO

For corporate passion to occur, the leader must deeply feel, communicate, and then rally a dissatisfaction with the status quo. He or she must keenly explain why the current situation is unsustainable or even unconscionable.

If a definition of leadership is basically moving others toward a goal—moving a group of people from one place to another—then the first part of our job as catalytic leaders is to define reality; it's a vital part of what we do. It's what Jesus did over and over for his disciples.

Catalytic leaders have to turn the heat up and help people understand why maintaining the present status quo isn't right or healthy and why inaction is not an option. The proverbial frog in the kettle on the stove doesn't realize how hot the water is becoming until it's too late and he's cooked; he didn't sense the danger of the current routine.

At some point, leaders sense that they can't stomach where they are anymore, nor their organization's apathy.

What can you *not* take anymore? Are you tired of a Christianity that has lost its hunger for more of the Kingdom of God? How dissatisfied are you with your own spiritual status quo? Jesus put it like this: "You're blessed when you've worked up a good appetite for God. He's food and drink in the best meal you'll ever eat."[38] A dissatisfaction with the status quo and desire for meaning affects all human beings at some point. But how we recognize it organizationally and lead through it is critical.

At the end of forty years of wandering in the wilderness after Israel's liberation from centuries of bondage under the Egyptian Empire, Moses receives a clear leadership command from God: "You have circled this mountain long enough. Now turn north…"[39]

The status quo was no longer acceptable. Israel's trek had been spotted with four decades of rebellion, disobedience, grumbling and divided loyalties. It was a spiritual status quo in desperate need of movement; as a matter of fact, the original generation that found change difficult to handle had died off.

Organizations (and leaders) must have a certain amount of change and challenge in order to be fully alive with new questions and decisions that force us to engage with God and his Kingdom more fully and deeply. Growth only comes from change.

In his seminal book, *Flow: The Psychology of Optimal Experience,* Hungarian author and psychologist Mihaly Csikszentmihalyi gives a fascinating account of a native North American tribe in British Columbia. He writes:

> The Shushwap region was and is considered by the Indian people to be a rich place: rich in salmon and game, rich in below-ground food resources such as tubers and roots—a plentiful land. In this region, the people would live in permanent village sites and exploit the environs for needed resources. They had elaborate technologies for very

---

[38] Matthew 5:6 (Message Bible)
[39] Deuteronomy 2:3 (New American Standard Bible (1995 Update)

effectively using the resources of the environment, and perceived their lives as being good and rich. Yet, the elders said, at times the world became too predictable and the challenge began to go out of life. Without challenge, life had no meaning.

So the elders, in their wisdom, would decide that the entire village should move…every 25 to 30 years. The entire population would move to a different part of the Shushwap land and there, they found challenge. There were new streams to figure out, new game trails to learn, new areas where the balsamroot would be plentiful. Now life would regain its meaning and be worth living. Everyone would feel rejuvenated and healthy.[40]

We are stimulated in life when there is a balance between anxiety and boredom, between low challenge and high challenge. The optimal state is what Csikszentmihalyi refers to as *flow*, a focused immersion in a task or activity that leaves one energized and in the zone.

Likewise with organizations: if left unattended or merely maintained, atrophy sets in resulting in apathy and complacency.

Csikszentmihalyi's *Flow Model* lays out the emotional outcome where challenge levels meet skill levels on low to high

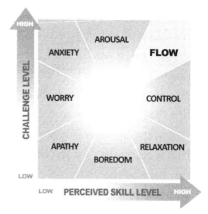

continuums. If a leader doesn't provide some heat or *direction* to the organization, mission drift occurs, and if left

[40] Mihaly Csikszentmihalyi; *Flow: The Psychology of Optimal Experience* (New York, HarperCollins, 2008), p.80

for too long a time, corporate deterioration sets in and in some cases is nearly irreversible—all that the future holds is a slow death.

At one point we purchased a demographic study based on a ten-mile radius of our church. It was filled with extremely helpful information derived from census material and several other surveys. One of the questions was a multiple choice response to a query about personal faith: "I am involved in my faith, I am somewhat involved in my faith, I have no faith involvement."

Within that ten-mile radius were approximately 667,000 people. Out of that number, nearly a half-million people reported they were only somewhat involved in their faith or had zero faith involvement. And honestly, I wasn't sure I believed the rest of them!

That's when I had an epiphany: we suck. After our leadership team laced our Diet Cokes with Zoloft and reviewed the stats, we decided to fearlessly evaluate and innovate our methods of evangelism.

Several months later when I downloaded this to the church one weekend, I said, "We can't be satisfied with the status quo. Not if we believe Jesus has the words to eternal life that begins now and carries into the age to come."

I went on to announce, "If you don't really believe that, then you ought to stop coming here and playing nice. We're not here to play religion or to make us feel good. If you just want to feel good, get some Two-Buck Chuck and rent a Will Farrell movie. Jesus didn't come to make you happy; He came to start a revolution and to transform lives, to give us significance, meaning, and power."

Leaders must guard against the comfortableness of the status quo. This wasn't about numbers, but if the reality of eternal destinations as described by Jesus and current injustices in our world doesn't affect us, something's wrong. If we believe that there are broken people all around us, if we believe that we have the antidote to a deadly disease called sin that's killing our fellow human beings...and yet we refuse to open our doors and hearts wider, then we have a huge problem with God. Jesus said that he came to *preach good news to the poor, proclaim freedom to the prisoners, recover sight for the blind, release the oppressed and proclaim the year of God's favor.*

John Scully recounts the legendary story of Steve Jobs courting him—then CEO of PepsiCo—to be the CEO of Apple. Scully tested him and asked for an outrageous salary, signing bonus and retirement. It was more than Jobs could realistically offer at the time, but he claimed that they would figure out a way to do it. Finally, Scully turned him down and said, "Steve, I'd love to be an adviser, but I don't think I can come."

Looking him in the eye, Jobs simply asked, "Do you want to spend the rest of your life selling sugared water, or do you want a chance to change the world?" Scully resigned from Pepsi-Cola and signed on to the fledgling computer company called Apple.

When Candy Lightner's thirteen-year-old daughter was killed by a drunk driver who had been arrested several times before, she discovered a problem bigger than her personal grief, loss, and pain: the lack of legislation to take people off the road who get hammered and then crawl into a two-ton weapon of sheet metal and gasoline. She formed Mothers Against Drunk Driving and in twenty-five years alcohol-related traffic deaths were reduced nearly forty-percent. An unfathomable tragedy and disgust with "that's just how things are" was a powerful impetus.

One last point on this status quo issue: I've observed that many organizations rarely create space for mavericks in their ranks. It's understandable: leaders may have gotten burned by pseudo-mavericks who are complainers and contrarians because of an agenda driven by a negative-oriented personality or a narcissistic need for recognition. But "loyal mavericks" are invaluable: they are devoted to the mission and vision of the organization and will raise a red flag when they sense there is a subtle drifting from the core values. Their dissension with conformity—which may have surreptitiously crept into the team—is guided by a commitment to the organization's health and mission.

In a healthy team, loyal mavericks feel safe in a truth-friendly environment that values risk-taking.

FIRESTARTER #2: PAINT A COMPELLING PICTURE OF THE FUTURE

The follow-up point is to create a compelling picture of the future, of what could be. For those of us in spiritual leadership, this has to ultimately come from God. But be sensitive to not paralyze the process by hyper-spiritualizing this: God may use your imagination or even a recognized "felt need."

The process of discovering a corporate vision may come as well from the imaginative, prophetic voice of your leadership team. But leaders have to drive the process and discovery.

For instance, you might have your key leaders imagine themselves ten years in the future writing a letter to a friend. Have them describe with as much detail as possible what they're excited about in their church or organization…what it looks like, what it's doing, what impact they're having on their community, what the atmosphere is like. As you later collate the letters, look for themes and commonalities. Is a picture emerging that you can synthesize and then offer back to the team for them to create an action plan to move toward it? But whatever process you use to create the driving dream for your organization, remember how critically important language is. Is it memorable, specific and simple? Wordsmithing is tedious but important; it can be handed over to another teammate to do, but you ultimately have to agree to it, believe it and live it. This is your number one job as it relates to the organization.

FIRESTARTER #3: COMMUNICATE THE VISION CLEARLY...AND OVER AND OVER

This brings us to the next organizational passion firestarter: communicate the vision clearly and repeatedly. Way more than you think. Key memory-sticking phrases are critical; they don't have to necessarily be clever or even original, but they have to be memorable.

Without a clear vision, your people have nothing to move toward...and nowhere to go. In the clever little book, *Alice in Wonderland*—written by a deacon, no less—Alice falls down a rabbit hole where she eventually asks the Cheshire Cat for directions.

"Would you tell me, please, which way I ought to go from here?"
"That depends a good deal on where you want to get to," said the Cat.
"I don't much care where—" said Alice.
"Then it doesn't matter which way you go," said the Cat.[41]

---

[41] Lewis Carroll; *Alice's Adventures in Wonderland* (New York, Millennium, 2014) p.33

What you're really driving is the non-manipulative process of *corporate vision ownership*. Nothing should thrill a leader more than overhearing a "private" in the organization describing the mission in a way that sounds as if they personally dreamed it up. That should never, ever threaten a leader—it's what you long for.

When people own a mission, their sense of responsibility is exponentially amped. But that movement to ownership often follows a typical adoption process. Understanding that process is crucial; it means that you have to be aware of the influencers and early adopters that are in your circles.

In his influential book *Diffusion of Innovations,* author, sociologist and professor Everett Rogers pioneered the study of how new technologies and ideas are absorbed by the masses…and graphed out the *Early Adoption Lifecycle.*

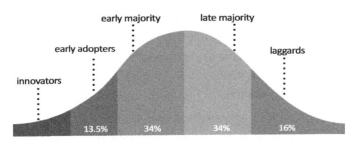

Rogers popularized the term *early adopters* to describe the people who take some risk in being the "guinea pigs" for what innovators create and publish. Early adopters are critical for any society or culture to evolve and progress from status quo contexts, particularly since they tend to be influencers, thought-leaders or trendsetters who through word-of-mouth may make or break an innovation.

Identifying and recruiting early adopters is a vital skill for leaders to learn. It can be done in conjunction with testing a vision's credibility. I'm not sure we're all as spiritually sharp as we'd like to be, and so testing out the veracity of a vision while identifying thought-leaders is not always typical for leaders. When I was first wondering about the creation of a place called the Healing Center that I thought God had suggested to me, I tested it out by talking about it with several different types of people and leaders. If their eyes brightened and they started talking about it in legitimately interested tones, then I knew we were on to something. It's been my best test for a vision's validity and identifying a potential early adopter.

The first time I presented the Healing Center concept to the whole church following a six-week series on poverty, they broke into applause at each of the four services—and then I reminded them that I'd be back in a year to ask them for a boatload of money.

That's when they got quiet.

That weekend a couple we had talked with briefly a few times before invited my wife and me to lunch after the last service. As we were eating our burritos and enjoying small talk and get-to-know-us chatter, they asked me to tell them more about the "Healing Center concept." I talked excitedly about the idea for a few minutes: how it could impact our city, how we could take a holistic approach to meeting people's needs, particularly the poor, and how it could introduce people who would never step into a church to the resources, beauty, and power of the Kingdom of God.

As we finished our meal, he leaned forward and said quietly, "I think this is a God-vision. I'd like to help you get started by giving you a million dollars as long as you keep it anonymous." I was stunned. I had never in my life imagined or even heard of anything like that…or that we even had people in our church that had that capability. I stuttered and thanked him and told him that I was frankly taken aback.

When my wife and I got into our car to drive home, we looked at each other and screamed, "No way!"

When I got home, I immediately emailed him and thanked him for his gift of one-zero-zero-zero-zero-zero-zero dollars. I wrote out six zeroes deliberately just in case he emailed back and said, "Dave, you dipstick. I didn't say one million; I said one hundred. Are you crazy?"

Instead, he responded simply with, "You're welcome."

I was in shock. It was much easier at this point to say to our trustees, "I think we have our seed money. Let's go for it!" That was the initial planning for a five-week series a year later to raise thirteen million dollars.

Today, the Healing Center has served thousands and thousands of people in our city, opening just as the recession hit and so many people lost their jobs. Cincinnati is continually ranked in the top ten poorest big cities in the United States in survey after survey. We have our hands full.

But the point is, if you have a big vision that requires serious financing, it's vitally important to meet with as many potential early adopters as possible. We had many, many "fireside chats" in our little ranch home with people in the church who had already been regular givers and investors in the mission.

And obviously, early adopters aren't just about capital campaigns; these are influencers of ideas and initiatives, people who have the ability to lead the largest segment on Roger's bell curve.

FIRESTARTER #4: PAY ATTENTION TO PROMPTINGS

Sometimes we simply need to be aware of promptings from the Holy Spirit. This is an "internal nudge," the inner whisper of the Spirit of God. It can come with a seemingly out-of-the-blue intuitive thought or impression, or a sudden imaginative picture.

A few years ago someone in the church asked me to have a coffee with two Nigerians he met who had started a small ministry in Jos, Nigeria. I honestly didn't know anything about Nigeria except for periodic emails informing me of an unclaimed inheritance waiting for me there.

I ended up meeting a fascinating person named Emmanuel Itapson who lived in the states and was an Associate Professor of Old Testament at Palmer Seminary in Philadelphia. He was accompanied by a friend, Patrick Dakum, who was the Director-General at the Institute of Human Virology in Abuja, Nigeria. They had helped form a fledgling organization to create micro-businesses in Nigeria.

It was a pleasant meeting at their request with no major agenda; I'm sure they wanted to network and perhaps hopefully get a little support down the road, though they never implied that. I didn't have anything in mind; I'd typically meet a lot of people from a lot of organizations that often wanted help and usually we frankly couldn't do much.

But this time as we were talking, out of the blue I sensed God whisper, "Go to Nigeria with these men." I was a little surprised and kept a poker face as the conversation continued. Embarrassingly, if you had shown me a map of Africa at that time, I probably couldn't have picked Nigeria out.

As they stood to leave, I asked Emmanuel if I could tag along the next time he went back to Jos, Nigeria. He looked a little surprised and asked, "What would you want to do?"

I said, "I'll carry your bags and just follow you around."

He smiled. "Oh no. I have to carry yours because you have white hair. We're taught to respect our elders!"

Whatever. We laughed, shook hands, said our goodbyes, and that was it. I think they left a little puzzled.

Four months later I was in Jos, Nigeria, taking two people from our church with me. Each day I would wake up a little puzzled after taking a bucket bath in a simple Nigerian home, asking, "Father, why am I here...six-thousand miles from home?" At the end of our nine-day trip, we met the paramount chief of the Rukuba tribe as he gathered his district chiefs in a rural concrete-block building with no electricity that day. He was outlining the top five things he wanted to accomplish for the nearly quarter-of-a-million people in the Rukuba tribe. At the top of his list was accessible clean water. The infant mortality rate in Nigeria was mind-boggling because of water-borne diseases.

He told a story of a diseased well in one village where they lost thirty to forty percent of the children in a matter of months. He wasn't the chief at the time and tried to tell the villagers it was because of the well but they wouldn't believe him. He tried to tear the well apart with his own bare hands but was restrained. I thought, "I like this guy; he's an activist!"

I found out later he had worked for the Nigerian State Department, had served as Ambassador to Scotland, and years earlier attended Oxford during former president Bill Clinton's time there. He was also a devoted follower of Jesus. He had retired and was recently elected chief of the tribe. He blew away all my stereotypes of tribal culture.

As he was talking about the water problem, I felt like my insides were vibrating. I thought about my own two girls: what if they had been born here? What if by some cosmic roll of the dice I had grown up in Jos and struggled to raise a family in a rural area where my kids walked for miles to get water? Just because I can turn a faucet knob in my kitchen that delivers clean, sparkling, drinkable water simply to wash dishes, what if God wanted to make us aware of the plight of our fellow sojourners on the other side of the planet?

I'm feeling all of this inside when I sensed God whisper, "This is why you're here. Somebody prayed in Jos, Nigeria…and I'm answering it now."

On the plane trip home, we began to dream. Instead of drilling a borehole or two for water in a couple of the villages, what if we bought a whole drilling rig, gave it to them in Nigeria, and let them drill dozens of boreholes? And what if it became a self-sustaining business/ministry model that enabled it to do the majority of wells for free?

When we got back to the Vineyard, I told the church, "Here's our new mantra: it takes a church to raise a village."

As a result, we launched the H_2O Nigeria water project. We gave one of our pastors, Kande Milano, the unenviable task of leading the massive project. She turned out to be a major hit with Nigerians because of the way her name was spelled, which turned out to be a common Nigerian spelling. And all because her mom in Germantown, Ohio thought it simply looked good on her birth certificate!

I don't think "Mama Kande"—as she became known in Jos—had even seen a drilling rig before. She began meeting with about fifty people who volunteered to be a part of the project: engineers, geologists, project managers, administrators, web-designers, construction workers and people who just wanted to help. For over a year they did all the research and connected with water specialists and organizations around the world and argued and debated and learned to work together…raising their own money to make the twenty-hour flight to Nigeria to see for themselves what needed to be done.

Eventually, the right rig was built, a truck was purchased, and a Nigerian board of directors recruited a drilling team. The drilling team consisted of five young men who were incredibly hard-working with degrees in engineering and hydrology. They were followers of Jesus and totally got that this wasn't just getting water out of the ground—this was about bringing the Kingdom of God.

Over the years, the team drilled over one-hundred life-saving wells primarily in the Plateau state of Nigeria.

That's the kind of thing that only God can do. And it all began with a simple Spirit-prompting that brought the best leadership out of dozens of people, here and across the pond.

FIRESTARTER #5: DO SOMETHING

"It had long since come to my attention that people of accomplishment rarely sat back and let things happen to them. They went out and happened to things."

Oft attributed to Leonardo da Vinci, this quote exemplifies the activistic nature of passionate leaders: sometimes you just need to do something. Anything. It's hard to steer a car when it's not moving. This doesn't sound very spiritual, but often people just want to see their church doing something meaningful.

In the fifteenth chapter of the book of Acts, Paul and Barnabas are spending time in Antioch teaching and training when Paul suggests that they go back through all the areas where they had planted churches on their first mission trip and see how they were doing. There's no indication that this was a heavenly-inspired plan; it seems as if out-of-the-blue Paul simply thought it would be a good idea to check up on their previous work, almost like a "do something/anything" moment. A practical idea and perhaps even dispassionately presented.

It turns out that he and Barnabas have a serious disagreement about whether to take a team member who had deserted them during their last trip. Tempers flare and they part company with Barnabas essentially heading south and Paul trekking north. It doesn't sound like a God-infused harmonious missional launch.[42]

But it's later on this trip that Paul has a dramatic vision during the night that would take him much further than his original plan, all the way to Greece. It was eventually an exhausting but incredibly fruitful trip. Had not Paul actively wondered about his previous work and some possible follow-up, this extended reach of the Kingdom of God might have never happened at that time. Sometimes it's best to simply do *something* that furthers the generalized plan of God.

Incidentally, it's really difficult to make a wrong or even stupid decision in the Kingdom of God if your heart is aimed at heaven with a desire to please God. He has the ability to redeem every decision; it's much less about geography than "heart ownership."

My friend Steven Manuel describes it like this: Suppose I go to my kid's room at bedtime and am puzzled to find him standing on his head. And suppose I ask him, "What in the world are you doing?" and he responds by declaring he's doing what he heard me tell him to do: "Go stand on your head." Steven then smiles and says, "No, I asked you to 'go to bed', not 'stand on your head'," and finds himself secretly thrilled at the idea that his son did what he *thought* his father

---

[42] Acts 15

asked. A heart of obedience is what the Father wants, the simple desire to please him. Obedience trumps clarity every time.

FIRESTARTER #6: CELEBRATE SUCCESSES

Leaders who are stoking the fire element and expressing passion for their organizational goals will typically gloss over this one. It may be that at this point their own adrenaline will drive them to take the next hill after a specific goal has been reached. But without some sense of celebration, followers will forget the purpose of a passionate appeal or initiative. Celebrating a success centers everyone on the true point of a particular initiative.

For healthy organizations that accomplish a specific objective, having a value celebrated through a personalized story is crucial. Not only does it remind everyone that a goal was accomplished, but it reinforces the idea that the organization is values-driven above all else. This is far more important than communicating a specific financial or numbers achievement.

What's more, this is critical not only after a final success, but during the process of accomplishing the goal. When we launched the capital campaign I referred to earlier, we asked everyone in the church to pray specifically what God might have them do financially and encouraged them that it wasn't about equal giving, but equal sacrifice. The reason why we referred to the three-year commitments not as equal gifts but equal sacrifice was because the word "sacrifice" forced us to see something in the future beyond our present needs-and-wants. In a very, very small way, it was no different than how Jesus saw the ultimate sacrifice: his own life. Or as he acquiesced, "Not my will...but yours, Father."

We wanted the church to understand that the joy for us would be seeing our city and our world change, that we were sacrificially giving in the present because of something we saw in the future.

During the five-week campaign, I received a powerful email that read in part:

> I thought you might want to hear my friend's story. Kelly is her name and she attends the Vineyard weekly with her five children, ranging from kindergarten to 8th grade, two of them with cystic fibrosis. Five years ago she called me to tell me her thirty-year-old husband had died the night before of a heart attack right in front of their children, while Kelly was holding their newborn baby.
>
> Recently she asked us how we plan to commit to the campaign. We shared a few ideas we have, as our finances are tight too, then she shared what God is putting on her heart. She had been asking God, "What can I do? You know how little we have." Kelly decided that since she has no extra cash, she could sell a piece of jewelry, not just any piece, but a special sentimental one Dan had given her years ago.
>
> What is her legacy? Not the jewelry, but the lives she can have a part of investing in…forfeiting a treasure that is priceless to her. Now *that* is someone I want to be like.

I cried when I received that email. Kelly's story was reminiscent of the comment Jesus made while watching people give an offering at the temple, particularly when the wealthy would ceremoniously drop a boatload in. But when an impoverished widow walked in and gave the equivalent of a few pennies, Jesus states implicitly that in the economy of the Kingdom of God, she gave more than all the others combined.

When I read part of that email to the church during the campaign, a revelatory reality-check fell on the church: a deep, challenging value was being expressed in that small "success story" of sacrifice. It became a convincing moment of conviction.

Don't forget to take the time to celebrate success at any level; it can light a fire of passion toward the mission and vision of your organization.

REFLECTION POINTS

On a scale of one-to-ten, how would you rate the current Fire|Passion level in your organization, church or ministry? What's your personal Fire|Passion level for your organizational mission, your people and the organization itself?

Do you have an intuitive sense of which of the six fire-starters you need to exercise in your church or organization? Is there one that you would typically lean toward? Reflecting on questions like these can be the first step to stirring up the Fire element in your own life and the people you lead.

Lack of passion can turn the best-intentioned churches into introverted, well-maintained bureaucracies. But beware: don't mistake passion for hype or use passion as the only means to get things done in your church. And one final caveat: bigger-than-life passionate personalities need bigger-than-life accountability systems for the long-term health of the organizations they lead.

The dark side of Fire|Passion is that it can overwhelm the absolutely critical element and relatively recent discovery in corporate-world leadership: servanthood. And that is what we shall explore next by examining the organizational-life-giving element of Water.

CHAPTER 4
WATER | SERVANTHOOD

Humble leaders inspire, but self-centered leaders
squash the spirit of the people.

~CHERYL BACHELDER

*"For even the Son of Man did not come to be served, but to
serve, and to give his life as a ransom for many."*

~JESUS

Water has long been associated with servant-hood. In Biblical times, it was the servant who offered water to thirsty guests and who washed their feet. In Isaiah's powerful, prophetic passage on the Suffering Servant who rescues and leads his people to freedom, he uses the metaphorical phrase "…he poured out his life"[43] as someone who is emptied out for the sake of others.

A servant-oriented leader clearly expresses and models the credo that "it's not about me." While they may carry a sense of destiny and calling, they keep that internal and deeply personal. Instead, they authentically communicate that the church, the mission and the mechanism are actually *more* important than them. They carefully guard their hearts and motivations by avoiding any semblance of entitlement or privilege. They bring energy to others and the vision rather than requiring or demanding it. They cultivate an outward-focus personally and in the organization they lead.

In 1970, Robert Greenleaf introduced the idea of *"servant leadership"* as a viable, critical component of leadership at any level. In his groundbreaking book of that title, he writes:

> The servant-leader *is* servant first. . . . It begins with the natural feeling that one wants to serve, to serve *first*. Then conscious choice brings one to aspire to lead. . . . The best test is: do those served grow as persons: do they, while being served, become healthier, wiser, freer, more autonomous, more likely themselves to become servants? And,

---

[43] "…he poured out his life unto death, and was numbered with the transgressors. For he bore the sin of many, and made intercession for the transgressors." Isaiah 53:12 (New International Version)

what is the effect on the least privileged in society; will they benefit, or, at least, not be further deprived? [44]

Greenleaf sums it up simply: the servant leader knows, "my success comes from your success."

TRUE SERVANTHOOD AND TRUE POWER

This Water|Servanthood characteristic of leadership is often considered a "soft" skill, juxtaposed with the hard-charging, my-way-or-the-highway style. But that's not actually a fair comparison. For instance, we might pit a Steve Jobs-style of leadership against a more collaborative, less confrontational style like James Sinegal, co-founder and former CEO of Costco. However, that's not exactly the defining difference in determining what servant-leadership is about. A case could certainly be made that Jobs was a servant of his vision for Apple; in his own words he would say that it was never about money, but rather building a lasting organization that had the ability to "change the world."

The problem is, every organization has to deal with the same common resource: people. And moving people toward a singular mission and a loyalty to it is as much art as science. Does the end justify whatever means? In Walter Isaacson's mesmerizing biography, *Steve Jobs*, we read an interesting perspective from one of the original Macintosh team members, Andy Hertzfeld:

> … *"The one question I'd truly love Steve to answer is, 'Why are you sometimes so mean?'" Even his family members wondered whether he simply lacked the filter that restrains people from venting their wounding thoughts or willfully bypassed it. Jobs claimed it was the former. "This is who I am, and you*

---

[44] Robert Greenleaf; *Servant Leadership: A Journey into the Nature of Legitimate Power and Greatness* (Mahwah, Paulist Press, 1977/2002), p.27

can't expect me to be someone I'm not," he replied when I asked him the question. But I think he actually could have controlled himself, if he had wanted. When he hurt people, it was not because he was lacking in emotional awareness. Quite the contrary: He could size people up, understand their inner thoughts, and know how to relate to them, cajole them, or hurt them at will.[45]

Author Isaacson offers his own perspective:

The nasty edge to his personality was not necessary. It hindered him more than it helped him. But it did, at times, serve a purpose. Polite and velvety leaders, who take care to avoid bruising others, are generally not as effective at forcing change. Dozens of the colleagues whom Jobs most abused ended their litany of horror stories by saying that he got them to do things they never dreamed possible. And he created a corporation crammed with A players.[46]

The point here is not to analyze whether Jobs was a servant-leader or not, but rather to bring a more nuanced definition: *the primary characteristics that highlight the water element of leadership are the lack of a sense of entitlement and the betterment of the followers in the pursuit of a vision.* Though Jobs at times seemed to be unconcerned about money, his modus operandi, according to his own hand-picked biographer, was thinking he was above the rules, from parking in the handicap spaces of his own company to the normal parameters of social engagement. Entitlement is a shape-shifter.

Author Scott Sinek articulates the danger of "entitlement creep" and how leaders can begin to feel arrogantly bullet-

---

[45] Isaacson, Walter (2011-10-24). Steve Jobs (Kindle Locations 9257-9265). Simon & Schuster. Kindle Edition.
[46] ibid (Kindle Locations 9257-9265)

proof in their decisions. In describing effective leadership, he writes:

> *(Leaders) are often willing to sacrifice their own comfort for ours, even when they disagree with us. . . . Leaders are the ones who are willing to give up something of their own for us. Their time, their energy, their money, maybe even the food off their plate. When it matters, leaders choose to eat last. . . . The leaders of organizations who rise through the ranks not because they want it, but because the tribe keeps offering higher status out of gratitude for their willingness to sacrifice, are the true leaders worthy of our trust and loyalty. All leaders, even the good ones, can sometimes lose their way and become selfish and power hungry, however. . . . What makes a good leader is that they eschew the spotlight in favor of spending time and energy to do what they need to do to support and protect their people.*[47]

Israel's difficult history in the Hebrew Bible is replete with leadership lessons, both good and bad. After King Solomon died and his complicated reign ended, his son Rehoboam was appointed king. The people of Israel found an audience with him and said simply that if he would ease the heavy taxation and overwhelming labor burdens his father had placed on them, they would faithfully serve him in his new royal role.

Rehoboam prudently asked for a few days to think about their request. During that time he sought consultation from the older advisors who had served his father. Their advice was straightforward: "If today you will be a servant to these people and serve them and give them a favorable answer, they will always be your servants."[48]

---

[47] Scott Sinek; *Leaders Eat Last: Why Some Teams Pull Together and Others Don't* (New York, Penguin Group, 2014), pp.66-67
[48] 1 Kings 12:7

The power and efficacy of establishing a servanthood leadership model was wisely viewed by experienced leaders as creating a culture of long-term relational productivity. Sadly, Rehoboam instead heeded the advice given him by the young men he had grown up with and who were now working for him. Their self-serving consultation was just the opposite: establish and define your leadership by telling Israel that you're going to be more harsh and demanding than Solomon ever was! It was a top-down, heavy-handed, controlling approach to leadership and productivity.

Rehoboam's decision was costly: a rebellion ensued and the nation of Israel was divided resulting in decades of resentment and wars, eventually leading to a disastrous diaspora.

THE SUBTLE CANCER OF "POWER ENTITLEMENT"

I've been mesmerized by crowd-sourced movements like the Occupy protests, the Tea Party movement, and the Arab uprisings. It didn't help to watch a particularly crazy person snag the media interview on your polarized news source of choice, or to buy into the short-sighted categories and simple labels like communists, ultraconservatives, fundamentalists, socialists, or whatever depending on the movement. But it's more than sociologically interesting when groups of people begin leveraging social media to tap into a simmering discontent. And then the tipping point comes.

Even apart from the politics and economics (let alone the moral implications), the blending of human nature, discontent and movements is intriguing. The fact is, any protest movement has to be listened to by the sheer fact that it reflects a repository of frustration. For example, even though the voice of Occupy was light-years from becoming monolithic, it reflected one thing clearly: a frustration with economic inequities mirrored by the widening gap between the rich and poor. But like other protests and movements, it believed leadership had a tin ear. We must tread carefully here: greed and covetousness can be equally practiced whether you're part of the 99 or 1%.

You may have agreed or disagreed with, for instance, the aims of Occupy or what the solution was—or even whether it elicited a solution (à la "let a free market settle it")—but the movement certainly reflected a perception. And we all know the fuzzy line between perception and reality.

In an article under the heading of *"Dear Wall Street, This Is Why The People Are Angry,"*[49] blogger and commentator Josh Brown self-identified as part of the Evil Empire, the "one-percenters," those who were vilified by the Occupy folks: Wall Street traders, bankers and stockbrokers who have been accused of controlling one-third of America's wealth. He's an investment advisor at Fusion Analytics in Manhattan.

> *In 2008, the American people were told that if they didn't bail out the banks, their way of life would never be the same. . . . At our darkest hour we gave these banks every single thing they asked for. We allowed investment banks to borrow money at zero percent interest rate, directly from the Fed. We gave them taxpayer cash right onto their balance sheets. We allowed them to suspend account rules and pretend that the toxic sludge they were carrying was worth 100 cents on the dollar. Anything to stave off insolvency. We left thousands of executives in place at these firms. Nobody went to jail, not a single perp walk. . . . People resigned with full benefits and pensions, as though it were a job well done.* [in subsequent court actions, two mid-level people were convicted.—author].

---

[49] APM's Marketplace website and radio show

The American taxpayer kicked in over a trillion dollars to help make all of this happen. But the banks didn't hold up their end of the bargain. The banks didn't seize this opportunity, this second chance to re-enter society as a constructive agent of commerce. Instead, they went back to business as usual. With $20 billion in bonuses paid during 2009. Another $20 billion in bonuses paid in 2010. And they did this with the profits they earned from zero percent interest rates that actually acted as a tax on the rest of the economy.

Instead of coming back and working with this economy to get back on its feet, they hired lobbyists by the dozen to fight tooth and nail against any efforts whatsoever to bring common sense regulation to the financial industry. Instead of coming back and working with the people, they hired an army of robosigners to process millions of foreclosures. In many cases, without even having the proper paperwork to evict the home-owners. Instead, the banks announced layoffs in the tens of thousands, so that executives at the top of the pile could maintain their outrageous levels of compensation.

. . . This is why they're enraged, this why they're assembling, this is why they hate you. Why for the first time in 50 years, the people are coming out in the streets and they're saying, "Enough."

No matter which side of the aisle you were on regarding TARP and the bailout, one thing is for sure: when leaders, whether they be political, economic, cultural or spiritual leaders, become or are perceived as entitled and myopic, people will eventually rebel. What were the trustees and boards-of-directors thinking when they karaoked to "Executives Gone Wild"…especially when those at the top were the ones ultimately responsible for tanking their own companies, save for the taxpayer bailout? Of course companies can do whatever they want to with their own money…that's part of how capitalism works. But how do you miss the obvious PR meta-message?

In the time it was published, Nick Hanauer's article in Politico was the most downloaded article for months. Similar to Brown's screed (Hanauer financially identified himself in the .01% wealthiest people in the U.S.), he aptly titled his post: *"The Pitchforks Are Coming...For Us Pluto-crats."*

Miguel De La Torre, associate professor of social ethics at the Iliff School of Theology in Denver, writes,

> *During the booming economy (1990 to 1995) when most corporations reported profit increases of up to 50 percent, the average CEO's pay rose from $1.9 million to $3.2 million, while the average worker, during that same time period, experienced a pay drop from $22,976 to $22,838.*

One of the purposes of the prophets in the Old Testament was to force the people with power and privilege to face the music. It shouldn't surprise us that there is an over-abundance of warnings given regarding the abuse of power and money. Over and over.

Jeremiah prophesied with the word of God:

> *"Doom to him who builds palaces but bullies people, who makes a fine house but destroys lives, who cheats his workers and won't pay them for their work, who says, 'I'll build me an elaborate mansion with spacious rooms and fancy windows. I'll bring in rare and expensive woods and the latest in interior decor.'"* [50]

Through Ezekiel, God cried out:

> *"The sin of your sister Sodom was this: She lived with her daughters in the lap of luxury—proud, gluttonous, and lazy. They ignored the oppressed and the poor. They put on airs and*

---

[50] Jeremiah 22:13–14 (Message Version)

lived obscene lives. And you know what happened: I did away with them." [51]

This really isn't a rip on the rich. Let's be honest: if you read Josh's blog on your own computer, you're among the estimated 6-7% elite of the world. But it seems to me that when a sizable group of people begins questioning the gap, someone needs to listen. Perhaps there is something to a "populous prophetic" voice. Of course, this is all somewhat relative when it comes to finances, but the warnings are out there when leaders, whether they be CEOs—or pastors—are perceived as being entitled.

The French Revolution is derided or cheered depending on your historical politics. It eventually produced Napoleon …and what a megalomaniac. Yet it was the self-consumed French aristocracy and the wealthy, powerful Church clergy who really missed it, and paid dearly with their heads. Literally. Though it's a dubious Marie Antoinette quote, *"Let them eat cake"* reflected the tone-deaf response to the populous when, among a barrage of other things, bread prices increased to a staggering fifty-percent of the average worker's wage.

Those at the top have a responsibility to be aware and respond wisely. If I were asked to give a little pastoral advice to CEO's and execs, it would be: don't ignore the rumble; a little self-restraint and self-discipline could go a long, long way. And we should all reread James' epistle.

Sharon Begley, Newsweek science editor and author of *Train Your Mind, Change Your Brain: How a New Science Reveals Our Extraordinary Potential to Transform Ourselves* writes,

---

[51] Ezekiel 16:49–50 (Message Version)

Power brings with it a sense of entitlement. The power-ful therefore feel entitled to break a rule or two even as they demand others follow the rules."[52]

This is where the New Testament turns this upside-down. Consider this: what if you had all the power in the universe? This is where we get a very different picture in the New Testament. In a remarkable passage in John's account of Jesus, the night before Jesus would die from an excruciat-ing Roman crucifixion, he gathers his disciples for a Passover meal. He knows these are his last hours with the ones who would carry his Kingdom-message to the world. If ever there was a time to dispense your most profound, critical instruc-tions, this was it.

Instead, we get this striking account:

> *Jesus knew that the Father had put all things under his power, and that he had come from God and was returning to God; so he got up from the meal, took off his outer clothing, and wrapped a towel around his waist. After that, he poured water into a basin and began to wash his disciples' feet, drying them with the towel that was wrapped around him.*[53]

In a matter of hours, Jesus would be arrested, dragged from place to place through a sleepless night, beaten, flogged until his torso was ripped to shreds, mocked, spit on, stripped, and nailed through the hands and feet to die a slow agonizing death. Would he not have had the right to say, "Hey, would you guys fix me dinner tonight? And how about a little respect? You have no idea what I'm about to go through. Don't you think it would be nice for you to wash my feet?"

Instead, he serves his leadership team.

---

[52] http://www.sharonlbegley.com/politicians-really-are-prone-to-hypocrisy
[53] John 13:3-5

As Jesus is washing his disciples' feet, Peter is noticeably disturbed. Perhaps he's picking up that if Jesus is really who he claims to be, it doesn't make sense for the Creator of the universe, the one who spoke galaxies into existence, who holds the world in place by his immense and incomprehensible power—is about to wash his feet. Peter senses that something is wrong with this picture.

So he asks, "Lord, are you really going to wash my feet? Seriously?"

Jesus enigmatic response is, "You're not going to get this now, but later it will make sense to you." He implies that serving our people creates long-lasting ripples that have a wider effect than we might understand.

A true leader is always a servant. Leadership is never seen as a self-esteem enhancer. A platform for influence is never held onto, it's not a white-knuckle ride. Effective leaders are servants. And they don't serve some mythical "out-there" folks—they serve the people they lead. Always.

I've always enjoyed taking prospective hires to a restaurant, primarily to create a more relaxed environment…but also to observe how they treat the servers. Not all servants are good leaders, but all good leaders are servants.

In the first century, the very religious Pharisee Saul was appalled by this fledgling cult of servants modeled after an itinerant rabbi from the wrong side of the tracks; they were worshipping a crucified Jesus of Nazareth as Lord and God. In order to protect the purity of his tradition, Saul's job was to legally and violently stamp it out.

But after his own dramatic conversion, Saul, who had now changed his name to Paul and suffering persecution for his newfound faith, wrote these stunning words from a jail cell:

Your attitude should be the same as that of Christ Jesus:
Who, being in very nature God, did not consider equality with
God something to be grasped, but made himself nothing, tak-
ing the very nature of a servant, being made in human like-
ness. And being found in appearance as a man, he humbled
himself and became obedient to death, even death on a cross![54]

From all the power in the universe...to a slave. The in-
carnation is a riches-to-rags story of supreme leadership to
accomplish a mission that has changed the lives of billions of
people worldwide over the last two millennia.

TEAM FIRST

Servant leadership—the water element—demands that
team development is vital. When it comes to achieving a
corporate mission, true servant-oriented leaders value a
team-based approach. The ability to do more and accomplish greater goals is achieved by coalescing the strengths of a
team. Elemental leaders live by the classic adage: imagine
what can be accomplished if you don't care who gets the
credit.

In *Organizing Genius: The Secrets of Creative Collabora-*
tion, leadership expert Warren Bennis writes:

> Our contemporary views of leadership are entwined
> with our notions of heroism, so much so that the distinc-
> tion between "leader" and "hero" (or "celebrity," for that
> matter) often becomes blurred. In our society leadership is
> too often seen as an inherently individual phenomenon.
> And yet we all know that cooperation and collaboration
> grow more important every day.[55]

---

[54] Philippians 2:5-8
[55] Warren Bennis; *Organizing Genius: The Secrets of Creative Collaboration* (New York, Basic, 1997), pg.1

Leaders today must lean more into empowerment rather than delegation, and values and direction over micromanagement.

At one point when Jesus was developing his team of disciples, he said simply, "The works that I do shall you do also...and even greater works," more than likely meaning that the power of the Holy Spirit would be exponentially multiplied through teams of "little Christs," Christians who would take the message of the Kingdom globally instead of being centered in one person in a dusty region of the Mideast. Imagine the surprise and encouragement that statement from Jesus would have been to the ragtag band of disciples who heard it.

Servant leaders stretch and challenge others, but within the context of encouragement. The word "encourage" simply means to inspire valor in someone else. The word comes to us from the French, based on the Latin word "cor"—meaning heart. It literally means "to give someone heart." To give courage to another is an essential part of being a leader; think of it as giving water to the thirsty soul of a team member.

IT'S NOT ABOUT YOU...

Jim Collins' best-selling classic *Good To Great* revealed fascinating data on leaders who had helped lead their organizations to sustained productivity and health. The gist of Collins' classic is this: over a period of several years, Collins and his team analyzed every company that had ever made the Fortune 500 (over fourteen-hundred companies throughout a thirty-year span). Based on criteria with tight parameters, only eleven qualified as moving from what they described as good organizations to truly great ones. Their research was focused on one central question: what causes a company to make the leap from being a good company to a great one and sustain it for at least fifteen years?

Collins gave the research team explicit instructions to downplay the role of top executives to avoid the simplistic "credit the leader" or "blame the leader" thinking common today. But the data uncovered something surprising. When their research eventually led them to study the CEOs of those eleven companies, an unanticipated pattern emerged. It wasn't the charismatic "rock star" leaders that made the difference. The good to great CEO's were an odd mix of true humility and professional will, or corporate resoluteness. Out of the study, Collins' team identified five stages of leadership, and all eleven companies had what they termed *Level 5 Leaders*, meaning they had successfully moved beyond four previous stages of leadership competencies.

Level 5 leaders were a fascinating paradox: "modest and willful," "humble and fearless." Or as Collins' put it:

> Level 5 leaders channel their ego needs away from themselves and into the larger goal of building a great company. It's not that Level 5 leaders have no ego or self-interest. Indeed, they are incredibly ambitious–*but their ambition is first and foremost for the institution, not themselves.*[56]

Collins would later write:

> Virtually everything our modern culture believes about the type of leadership required to transform our institutions is wrong. It is also dangerous. There is perhaps no more corrosive trend to the health of our organizations than the

---

[56] Jim Collins; *Good to Great: Why Some Companies Make the Leap...And Others Don't* (New York, HarperCollins, 2001), p.21

rise of the celebrity CEO, the rock-star leader whose deepest ambition is first and foremost self-centric.[57]

As a matter of fact, as soon as a CEO began doing book promotions and appearing on talk shows, it was over.

Servant-leadership is most effective when combined with clear visionary communication and expectations. Don't confuse the servant leader with being mousy or afraid to take charge. While Jesus is often portrayed as a soft-skill leader as he related to his team ("Greater love has no man than this that he lay down his life for his friends"), he was absolutely resolute in his mission and frequently confronted his team with hard-edged truths about themselves and their focus toward that mission.

LEARNING TO LEAD LIKE JESUS: THE ULTIMATE SERVANT

When the Vineyard Cincinnati Church began to grow, the style of how ministry was conducted was clearly being embedded in our DNA: we would operate like a business, rather than a family. After all, we were all peers, so there was no "father figure"-type leader. Some of us had been a part of churches that functioned like a mom-and-pop operation and frankly were often managed poorly. We were not going to have a "family"-style of church leadership. As a matter of fact, many of us came from dysfunctional families, so why emulate that in the organization? Who wants that as a model? Instead, it would be run like a business, with clear objectives, goals, strategies and measures. What's more, we knew there would be times when the organization would outgrow the abilities and capacities of some of the people from time to time.

---

[57] http://www.jimcollins.com/article_topics/articles/the-misguided-mixup.html

The tension between relationships and mission often plays out in how leaders balance process with results, sometimes pitting staff development against goal-achievement. In our case, we definitely leaned toward the latter. And in our defense, the church was moving and growing so fast we were simply running to keep up and felt we needed smart self-starters who required little oversight.

But there was something subtler, more subliminal, beneath that.

Of course every leader wants a team of rock stars. If someone becomes detrimental to the mission and pace of the organization, it makes sense to ask them to step aside: the organization and mission are too important. This becomes more difficult, though, when these people are our friends and we're emotionally invested in them. As a result, we began developing an emotional "arms-length" distance from our direct reports and staff. With that self-protective approach, we secretly reasoned it would be easier to deliver a lackluster performance review—or even fire someone—if they weren't performing well. The emotional distance would keep the pain to a minimum; we would feel a little safer with our hearts at a distance.

At one point, I recognized this in myself and began to seriously question how Jesus did this leadership-thing. What would it look like to truly emulate a Jesus-style of leadership? Was it possible…or too idealistic?—after all, he had a cosmic leg up as the Son of God. You have to admit that's a slight advantage.

Jesus seemed to approach this from a totally different angle: What if the intimacy/friendship level of the relationship was heightened? What if trust became so expansive that just the opposite effect happened? When we, as leaders, had to say the tough things to someone, would we be given grace and a more receptive heart in which to speak?

What was evident was this: he seemed to be just the opposite of the "arms-length" school. He was highly invested and spent an inordinate amount of relational time with his team. He modeled ministry life to them; he walked with them, ate with them, camped with them, went to dinner parties with them, and even called them his friends.[58]

It's certainly rare in leadership circles to hear a CEO or even a pastor refer to his or her staff as their friends. I have an acquaintance who served on a leadership team at a church where the senior pastor never spent a single "off-the-time-clock" minute with him—he had never once been invited to the pastor's house after official work times. A while back I read in a Forbes blog this typical bit of managerial advice: "Make it a rule to not fraternize with your employees, and choose your partners wisely."[59]

Absolutely choose your partners wisely; Jesus spent a night in prayer before choosing from all of his disciples, possibly hundreds at that time, twelve in which he would invest his time, energy and deepest teachings. But not fraternize with them?—that would be impossible in a Jesus-leadership style.

As tight is their friendship was, Jesus would still look at Peter at one point and say, "You're in league with the devil, Peter, and have replaced God's plans with your own. Get out of my sight."[60]

Imagine the shock and disappointment Peter must have felt. It was even said in front of the management team. And

---

[58] Luke 12:4; John 15:13-15
[59] http://www.forbes.com/sites/martinzwilling/2011/09/28/10-mistakes-growing-companies-routinely-make/
[60] Matthew 16:23

all Peter had expressed was concern about Jesus' referencing his own death.

But the power of that moment was this: even though Jesus handed a harsh and difficult critique to Peter, their relationship had so much depth and breadth that Peter continued to follow Jesus' leadership and wasn't blown out of the water. The investment Jesus had made over time in Peter's development softened the blow of truth. Or as the proverb says, *"Wounds from a friend can be trusted..."* [61]

Leadership requires speaking the truth about the organization's productivity and about people's abilities and capacities—but with genuine love for the leaders and workers you serve with. This isn't a mushy, idealized picture of leadership, but a reflection of the most amazing leader that ever walked the planet.

The Water|Servanthood approach is about learning how to speak the truth...but with genuine love. As a matter of fact, Paul claims that the universal spiritual organization known as the Church—which has a clearly defined mission—functions best as it interdependently operates by love. [62]

OTHERS FIRST

I once posted this question online: "If you've ever had a boss or manager that you enjoyed working long, hard hours for, what made him or her worth working that hard for?" I received a barrage of fascinating answers and comments.

Certain themes emerged, but one stood out to me. Generalized, it was: they noticed me. My work, my contribution, my hours. There was genuine appreciation. And it was

---

[61] Proverbs 27:6a
[62] Ephesians 4:15-16

stated over and over that they felt their boss was "in the trenches with me." That means at an emotional level as well.

Which reminded me of the need for bosses to often subjugate their own needs to the service and needs of their people in order to accomplish a higher mission. We have an intriguing story of a fascinating leader in history who wrestled with this: it's the telling story about King David in the Old Testament. And as an aside, it inadvertently contributes to the street cred of the historicity of the Bible because it exposes its heroes as real, vulnerable and, at times, messy leaders. If I had written it, I would have made the heroes look better. Peter really should have fired his publicist.

David's family is a case study in dysfunction. After one particularly ugly family matter, David wouldn't speak to his own son Absalom for two years even though they lived in the same town. As a matter of fact, David wouldn't even look at him. It wasn't a "family values" success story.

Years later, Absalom staged a coup against his own father. It began simply: with a huge entourage in front of him, Absalom would get up early and stage himself along the street to the courthouse. While people came for their court case, he would stop them and ask about their troubles. Listening with feigned concern and empathy, he would respond, "Wow. You know, if I were the king, I'd make sure you had good representation and were treated fairly. There's no justice in this freakin' city."

And when people approached him and bowed before him—after all, he was the king's son—he would lift them up and kiss them, offering a sign of friendship and trust. In short order, it reads that "he stole the hearts of the men of Israel."

Absalom ultimately overtakes Jerusalem and the mighty King David—the giant-killer, the warrior-poet who had songs written about his exploits, who defended Israel in countless wars from aggressive nations, the king anointed by the great prophet Samuel—was forced to run like a scared dog from his own son. Absalom even sexed it up with his father's servants on the top of the house so all Israel could see. It was an utter slam against his dad. The whole story is filled with spiritual and psychological intrigue and revenge.

But eventually there was an intense battle between David's army (the loyalists) and Absalom's followers (the insurgents). Over twenty-thousand men were killed in a bloody civil war, but David's army prevailed. David had asked the general of his army, Joab, to be careful to capture his son Absalom alive, but it doesn't pan out well. Joab was so angry that Absalom had created such havoc and loss of lives that he killed Absalom. David's men won at a high cost in an exhausting victory.

But when news got back to David about the victory, he was only concerned for his son. When he heard that Absalom had been killed, he was shaken and wept publically: "My son, my son. If only I had died instead of you!"

How emotionally debilitating that would have been for the national psyche of Israel and the returning vets. What should have been celebrated as a victory with Jerusalem spared from a self-consumed, narcissistic leader, instead, the beloved King David was overwhelmed with grief and had lost his "leadership objectivity." The effect was so destructive that it reads in 2 Samuel 19:2, "And for the whole army the victory that day was turned into mourning..."

But I love what Joab did. He had just led a huge military victory at great risk to himself and his men, but what he did next could have certainly guaranteed his death at the hand of the king.

Joab went to the king and said frankly,

> *"Today you have humiliated all your men, who have just saved your life and the lives of your sons and daughters and the lives of your wives and concubines. You love those who hate you and hate those who love you. You have made it clear today that the commanders and their men mean nothing to you. I see that you would be pleased if Absalom were alive today and all of us were dead. Now go out and encourage your men. I swear by the Lord that if you don't go out, not a man will be left with you by nightfall. This will be worse for you than all the calamities that have come upon you from your youth till now."* So the king got up and took his seat in the gateway. When the men were told, "The king is sitting in the gateway," they all came before him...*[63]*

They *all* came before him.

They needed to be, they *wanted* to be, encouraged and inspired by their leader. Noticed. They needed to know that their sacrifice was recognized by him. They wanted to know that he was still passionate for the kingdom, their kingdom. They needed his leadership.

Frankly, there are times when leaders are required to compartmentalize things. Good leaders are especially aware of this. And by leaders, I mean anyone who has some responsibility for someone else at some level. A parent. A manager. An older brother. A committee chair. A teacher. Everyone has someone who is watching them.

Joab was "leading up." He reminded David that something bigger was at work here. That David, as a leader of the nation in this critical time, had to compartmentalize his grief

---

[63] 2 Samuel 19:5-8a

and his needs and deal with that at another time. But it was necessary in that moment to submit his personal pain to a passion for something bigger than himself—the kingdom, for the good of others.

A leader has personal issues and mission issues that have to be reconciled on a regular basis, and both have to be given space and dealt with appropriately. But true servant-hood is about something more than our personal needs and wants. This is a "dying-to-self" that all healthy leaders understand. You find it in Jesus' words and Paul's writings.

ROLLING OUT THE RED CARPET

Finally, let's unpack the most pragmatic and, I believe, highest spiritual corporate expression of the Water|Servant-hood element.

One day Jesus announced a simple but sweeping state-ment (and narcissistically insane if he wasn't who he said he was) about his purpose in life: *"For the Son of Man came to seek and to save what was lost."*[64] Bold and beautifully fo-cused.

But after he was crucified, his closest disciples were hud-dled behind locked doors on Sunday night, fearing for their lives and clueless regarding their mission. After all, this was the leader on whom they had pinned their hopes. There was no Plan B. Now their lives were endangered and this new little sect of Judaism was primed to whimper out.

Suddenly, Jesus appears in the room in a new type of body, fully alive. And, of course, the disciples freak. He shows them the wounds in his hands and side, reassuring them that he was indeed real after offering the obligatory

---

[64] Luke 19:10

"this-is-a-transrational-panic-inducing-experience-but-don't-be-afraid" greeting: *"Peace be with you."* [65]

Then he gives them a mission on which to spend the rest of their lives: *"As the Father has sent me, I'm sending you."* Just as he was sent into the world on a search-and-rescue mission, he now gives them that same mandate. And in some odd pre-Pentecost experience, he breathes on them, commanding them to receive the Holy Spirit. They now clearly had their mission and the empowered chutzpah to do it.

And just as he had with his disciples, they—and therefore we—were to develop students (disciples) who were outward-focused and servant-oriented in their ministry philosophy and therefore to be (super)naturally broken for "lost" people.

From the earliest days of our church's beginnings, one of the primary things we worked hard at developing was a servant-oriented culture. We believed strongly that serving others was a powerful vitamin for spiritual and mental health—moving from an inward-focus to an outward-focus.

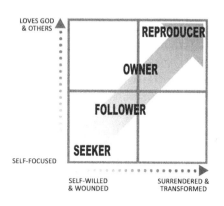

DISCIPLESHIP MATRIX

As I mentioned in chapter two, we later defined a disciple very simply as: *a surrendered and transformed person who loves God and others.*

If we graph that definition into a matrix, spiritual growth is moving forward on the bottom axis from being *self-willed*

---

[65] John 20:19

and wounded to *surrendered and transformed* and along the left side from being *self-focused* to *loving God and others.* The obvious ideal is to hopefully function in the upper right quadrant as much as possible.

What's more, when we lay the basic "life-stages" of a healthy believer on top of that—from being a (1) seeker of God to (2) a follower of Jesus to (3) deeply owning our faith to (4) a reproducer of the life of Jesus in others—it's easy to recognize that authentic spiritual health is a progression from an inward to an outward focus. Part of our job is to help people self-identify where they are and have a clearer picture of where they're going and who God wants them to be.

Christian philosopher C. S. Lewis observed what that might actually look like in person:

> Do not imagine that if you meet a really humble man he will be what most people call "humble" nowadays: he will not be a sort of greasy, smarmy person, who is always tell-ing you that, of course, he is nobody. Probably all you will think about him is that he seemed a cheerful, intelligent chap who took a real interest in what *you* said to *him*. If you do dislike him it will be because you feel a little envious of anyone who seems to enjoy life so easily. He will not be thinking about humility: he will not be thinking about himself at all.[66]

To reiterate, why did Jesus come? In his own words, "to seek and to save what was lost." The "lost" are you and me and all our reprobate friends and neighbors and families. Or more specifically, everyone on Planet Earth. And in what way did he send us?—in the same way the Father had sent

---

[66] C.S. Lewis; *Mere Christianity* (New York, HarperCollins, 2001), p.128

him: authorized with a mission and empowered by the Spirit.

If there are any doubts that this is our prime mission, think about this: in heaven, the Church gathered there is worshipping. In heaven, the Church is creative. And in the future new heaven and new earth, we'll eat together, play together and fellowship together...just like the Church currently on earth. But the one thing the Church in heaven cannot do is bring lost children home to the Father. What must that difference tell us about the priority of the Church's business here?

It is through redeemed people that the Kingdom and the *missio dei* advances. In his book *The Kingdom Conspiracy*, Scot McKnight (quoting Tim Dickau) describes the mission as moving people:

+ from isolation to community towards radical hospitality;

+ from homogeneity to diversity towards shared life among cultures;

+ from charity to friendship towards seeking justice for the least;

+ from the confrontation of idolatries to repentance towards new life in Christ.[67]

I would posit that all four aspects of that mission are summed up by moving people from *outside* the Kingdom to *inside* the Kingdom and embracing its values and mission (community, shared life, justice). Of course, that means being introduced and surrendering to the King of that Kingdom, for wherever there is a Kingdom there is a

---

[67] Scot McKnight; *Kingdom Conspiracy: Returning to the Radical Mission of the Local Church* (Grand Rapids, Brazos, 2014), p.139

King...and conversely, there is no real King without the people the King rules.

Therefore, it appears that inviting people to connect with the True King is the Church's first priority...and the ultimate expression of true servanthood.

There are two ways to accomplish that: we either *attract* them or we go *find* them. And if we do this in the context of a community of believers, we either create environments designed to attract people and/or we develop missional or incarnational communities embedded in the area that we want to reach. And frankly, both approaches are closely joined at the hip.

Let's think both/and for a few moments.

Consider your own neighborhood. When you first moved into your neighborhood, you probably didn't knock on your neighbors' doors to tell them they needed to repent. More than likely, you began informal conversations while cutting the grass or washing your car. And then perhaps you invited them over to grill out. Maybe you took a big risk and even started an "explorers" Bible study. Regardless, you thought about your environment—probably straightened up the house, vacuumed, cleaned the bathroom, baked some great smelling brownies or picked up some wine and brie. Whatever. You invited them into your family's emotional field.

In many ways, you were first wanting to win them to yourself...so they might know you're fairly normal and to earn enough relational capital to share the most important thing in life: how God's story is intersecting theirs.

It wasn't about making them an evangelistic project. That's creepy. But it *was* all about love; you were genuinely caring for them...and motivated by the Holy Spirit to share the Best News of the Universe: that God loves them and is offering amnesty...that heaven has invaded earth.

But what never fails to baffle me is how rarely many church leaders give a moment's thought about the *atmosphere* of their church environments. Or their church's *culture* and how that's expressed. After all, they're inviting people into their "family's" emotional field.

The fear is that if they lean into the attraction side, they're feeding into the pervasive consumeristic culture of the world. But think about all the people who came to Jesus looking for something specific: physical healing, food, a cause, community, hope, validation, redemption. In a broad sense, we're all consumers at different depths of needs and wants. He didn't always give them what they wanted—for example, the rich young ruler,[68] multiple Pharisee encounters,[69] the initial interaction with the Canaanite woman[70]— they nevertheless felt safe enough to approach him. If that's our approach, then crucial aspects like hospitality, atmosphere, language and the delicate balance between invitation and challenge are tensions we live with. Jesus' demeanor, his mind-bending parables, his ability to interact with the common—and sometimes seemingly irreligious—person, caused him to attract people to himself.

On the other hand, he also moved from city to city finding others to present his Kingdom message.[71] Again, he said he came to "*seek*…that which was lost." If you opt for *finding*—or seeking—rather than *attracting*, that means that the purpose of your primary weekend gathering is for worship and equipping. Therefore, a key part of your discipleship system is teaching your people how to evangelize and then assessing how effective they are beyond the

---

[68] Matthew 19:16-22
[69] Matthew 12:38-39
[70] Mark 7:26-27
[71] Mark 1:38

church building walls in order to know if your system is actually working. It's obviously necessary to get real data to honestly evaluate the training and, equally important, know if people are being assimilated into the Body of Christ. Frankly, I have a difficult time seeing evangelism apart from community.

I think a more sensible approach is to utilize both *attraction* and *finding*. There will always be some creative tension in either method, but let's unpack one of the two.

The question to start with is: what's the invitational and attractional factor of your weekend gatherings? But that implies you have to first ask: what's the purpose of your weekend services? Church leaders have to define that. There's not necessarily a right or wrong answer, but it must be defined.

In the American culture, if unchurched or dechurched people are going to explore the faith, it typically means checking out a church...and Sunday morning is the most obvious time. If that's the context in which Christians are inviting others or the perceived "prime time" for people to explore Christianity (this often happens during the late teenage years to early twenties, or when couples begin the life-altering experience of having children), then church leaders need to think hard about what that means to them.

WHAT'S YOUR VIBE?

Decades ago we determined that God wanted us to shape our weekends to be a safe place to hear the dangerous message of Jesus. We became very intentional. We wanted to lower all the religious and sub-cultural barriers that got in the way of people hearing the essential message: God is crazy in love with you, but to really experience that love you'll have to surrender…and die.

Therefore, in that light, the atmosphere of the weekend environments is critical. Or the *vibe.*

Vibe is a term jazz musicians used for years about the *feel* music has to have. It's all about atmosphere…it's what others feel as you do business. You can play the right notes with the coolest players on the best equipment, but not have a vibe. It just doesn't feel right. Vibe is critical; without it, someone can throw a party with all the right elements— food, friends, and music—and it still not work. When the party is more draining than energizing, it's a drag; and chances are good guests will avoid the next party at that place.

Every organization has a vibe. Families have a vibe. You can spend a few minutes in a home and quickly pick up that this family does not have a lot of fun together…or this family is so unstructured nothing is ever accomplished…or so structured that creativity is choked. If the atmosphere is such that I prefer not visiting that house again, I would say there is no vibe, or at least a good one.

Every church has a vibe as well. The atmosphere is charged with something…or nothing. The hard part is actually identifying the vibe.

As we explored in chapter two, organizations from billion-dollar companies to churches often have little self-awareness. Why does the organization exist?

I had a relative who was frustrated and entrenched in a dying church (in a large metropolitan area) of twenty-five people mostly over the age of sixty. Many years earlier they had lost their way and self-awareness and had slowly dwindled down to a handful of elders who had no desire to change. Eventually, the church was closed, sold and bull-dozed over for a new subdivision.

Strategic church leaders must come to a place where they answer two philosophical (but extremely pragmatic) questions for their organizations: who are we and why are we here? They take their people through difficult times and changes to fulfill their purpose as an organization.

If these questions are not asked, they'll keep plugging in the latest and greatest trendy program to try to make something happen. Be careful: one can't take any particular program and plug it into their model without looking at the attachments. Great programs are attached to great values. It seems to me that the idea of adopting a model only works to a certain degree. Churches have personalities like human beings: to want to be just like someone else is disastrous—and God will break us in that process in order to create what *he* wants, which boils down to a dependency on him.

That doesn't mean that adopting a model is altogether wrong. In fact, it is actually part of the growth process for a church. Musicians learn to play by first emulating the artists they love. Budding guitarists will copy the licks and riffs their guitar hero makes until they eventually find their own voice. Or just as a child imitates its parents, as she approaches her teenage years, there is a reassessment and questioning of authority, models, and values.

So it is with a church. What's more, I think that every pastor/leader goes through a breaking process as well. There is a "nervous breakdown" point, an angry, frustrated point where one makes hard decisions concerning what they are *for*. The end result may *be* the original model, but it will be based on different values, I can assure you.

People will pick up the vibe of your church primarily from one place: your weekend services. And so when thinking about the weekend services of your church, I would consider five essential "vibe intangibles":

1. Participation;
2. Energy;
3. Inclusiveness;
4. Quality;
5. Flow.

PARTICIPATION

Are people engaged during the service? Are they actively listening while the speaker offered his or her message? Do they respond in some way during worship? Is there any attempt by your leadership team to assess people experiencing God in some tangible way? Is there any laughter during the teaching (humor is a big deal: it's a major indicator of icebreaking. I would jokingly tell our creative team, "Theology is easy; comedy is hard.")? Are people invited in any way to respond to or receive the Good News? Are people given an opportunity to connect further with the church and in some measurable way? On a scale of one-to-ten, how would you honestly rate the level of participation? Even if the weekend service is a highly produced presentation, it still has to provide an opportunity for people to feel as though they were engaged in some way.

ENERGY

Is there a sense of momentum…that the service is going somewhere? Are the worship songs directed to God? Does the music feel more like a dirge than a celebration? Do people on the platform (worship leaders, welcome host, teaching pastor, whomever) appear warm, authentically energetic, and informal…or cold, bored, disingenuous or cheesy (even if you personally know they're not like that)? Are the messages inspirational and challenging in some way? On a scale from boring or irrelevant to a call-to-action or soul-touching, how would you rate the average message? Is there often some sense of the presence of God during the services?

INCLUSIVENESS

Is the language used during the service culturally sensitive and inclusive or too "inside" and filled with buzzwords and Christianese? Are the announcements strictly for "family insiders"? Are the words to songs easily accessible as well as understandable? Is the room lighting typically appropriate (allowing for some anonymity yet warm and inviting)? Are there enough descriptions and explanations of the order of the service? Is there culturally-inclusive music before and after the service? How does your hospitality team come off?—on either end of the spectrum, were they busy talking with each other or desperately targeting people like an aggressive salesperson? Do your services appear authentically transparent? Would people attending for the first time see people who "are like me"—and not just in a token sense, but in roles of visible leadership?

QUALITY

Does the overall weekend service reflect an expression of your best efforts for your guests? Do the sermons/messages seem unresearched and off-the-cuff rather than thoughtfully developed for maximum comprehension and relevance? Do the print or video graphics look like a third-grader's Power-Point book report? How are the worship leader's abilities rated on a scale from unprepared or distractingly poor to confident and genuinely worshipful? Does he or she have a warm rapport or seem remote and spiritually weird? How does the worship band appear: bored or like they just woke up? Do they sound like they picked up their instrument for the first time that morning? How is the sound quality? Does the facility look dirty and uncared-for? How would you rate your first-impressions?

FLOW

Does the typical weekend message seem like it has continuity and connection from point to point? Are there rabbit trails? Does it feel too long, rambling, and redundant? Great communicators can handle 35-45-minute talks, but most of us could cut the fluff and have way better messages by keeping them no longer than twenty-five minutes. And here's a little buzzkill: really great communicators are few and far between. How many athletes make it to the Olympics? Face it: there are only a few Andy Stanleys. How long was the overall service (if you want to know how long it should be, ask your volunteers in the nursery—you'll get an earful)? Did people leave wanting more (that's a good sign)? Was the order of the service paced well? Was there a sense of continuity with each part? Did the worship leader talk/preach between songs? (Stop it. Please.) How long were the announcements?—people automatically tune out during this part. Why torture them? Do the services seem connected thematically (Really?—an up-tempo "happy" song after a heavy message on crucifixion?)? Do things feel disjointed?

Of course, these five intangibles are subjective. But as a leader, you have to begin to benchmark them against what you want to achieve in creating invitational environments. If you don't create and protect the vibe, believe me: someone else in the church will.

For an outside perspective, offer an unchurched neighbor, friend or someone you met at Starbucks twenty-five dollars to visit your church with the condition that he or she be honest and tell you afterward what they actually felt and experienced: Did they feel welcome? Did it feel clique-ish? Did it seem weird to them? Were they bored? Did they feel singled out? Were they able to find the restrooms? How was the signage? Did the message or music connect with them at all? Etcetera, etcetera.

Or ask a volunteer to take their smartphone and video everything from driving into the parking lot to leaving the facility…then look at it with your leadership team. You may be shocked. Years ago we did and noted, for instance, there was no signage for our free coffee to let newcomers know it was actually free. That could be a simple, but uncomfortable, little barrier.

It's worth mentioning that the Greek word we translate as *hospitality* in the New Testament literally means *love of strangers*. At the very least, how welcome do strangers feel in your weekend services? Do you come off as indifferent…or equally bad, desperate? Hospitality is only one aspect, but you have to take an honest look at the invitational-factor of your services: why are your people not inviting others to their church—especially if the best salesperson is a satisfied customer?

I don't mean your weekend service has to be The Big Show—personally, I'm not into that. It just needs to be authentic, warm and accessible to your community.

But the other thing to consider is: how are these five intangibles expressed and delivered? The main ways those vibe indicators are shaped are by four drivers (in no particular order):

1. the style and personas of your primary presenters
2. the expressed values of the church
3. your theology
4. the permissible presence of God

Let's touch on each of these.

DRIVER #1: THE STYLE AND PERSONAS OF YOUR PRIMARY PRESENTERS

Your primary presenters/communicators are the visible "up-front" people: worship leaders, hosts, musicians, announcement-givers, offering takers, teaching pastors, senior pastors, and so on—whoever gets up on the podium or stage on a weekend. It's amazing what people pick up about your church simply by who you put up in front of them, not to mention all the non-verbals they intuitively catch.

For instance, in our early days, it was important to me to have a particular tatted-up-long-haired musician in the worship band: it made the statement that anyone could come to this church…even those whom "churched-people" or religious-conservatives might have shunned back in the day. To people who were wary of rejection from the church, his presence announced: you are welcome here. The motto we were using in the late 1980's and putting on our bumper stickers was: *Come as you are…you'll be loved.* That approach seemed to us to mimic the heart of Jesus who was referred to as the "friend of sinners."

But it goes beyond appearance. We also discovered that unchurched people looked for certain personality aspects—for instance, transparency. It's good to self-disclose—

particularly when it is connected with humor. It reveals honesty in a way that says "I don't take myself too seriously; *my relationship with God* I take seriously." We went out of our way to poke fun at ourselves as pastors.

Do the people you put up front come off harsh...or bored...or phony? This isn't a matter of only offering the microphone to the bright and beautiful... because that can come off as canned or staged. But it is important to consider the personality and vibe that the person gives off. Do they come off condescending? Judgmental? Indifferent? Does their nervousness make others uncomfortable? Does it make an implicit statement about who is welcome here...perhaps diversity-wise?

Who do you put up in front of people? It's important as a leader to be intentional and not just leave it to chance. Seriously. Or think of it like this: if your son or daughter married someone from a different race, would you let your outspoken bigoted uncle give the wedding toast? I don't think so. It's important to manage who you give the microphone to if you care about people.

DRIVER #2: THE EXPRESSED VALUES OF THE CHURCH

What are the actual values of your church...and how are they being expressed? We communicate our values by what we choose to talk about and what we measure. For instance, if I said that as a church we existed to love God and others, but the first metric I asked the staff for on Monday was our offering count, it's clear that the staff will assume what I really value is financial stability. And while that's an important indicator of healthy growth and discipleship, it's up to the leader to communicate and express the strongest values in the organization…and if it's not people, you're in the wrong business.

DRIVER #3: YOUR THEOLOGY

Your "experienced theology" creates the climate of your services. For instance, at Vineyard Cincinnati, we had a strong emphasis on grace. We understood that the concept of grace, as displayed in the giving of God's Son, is deeply unique to Christianity. That means that Jesus Christ's redemptive work in us did not make us valuable to God; the fact is we were already so valuable to God even in our depravity that he sent the most precious and perfect gift to purchase us. To God, we were the pearl of great price, worth everything to obtain for himself. This incarnate aspect of God gives us tremendous freedom to accept people, to be *with* them.

Because of this incarnate theology of grace, it created a desire to reduce the sub-cultural barriers between us who have encountered God's redemption and those who haven't. For instance, decades ago, that approach drove us to be casual in our style and dress and reduced one less barrier for someone attending church. Our preaching and speaking style was laid-back and relaxed, filled with life applications and challenge, interspersed with illustrations, humor and self-disclosing stories to break up the message into more accessible pieces.

Time is our current culture's currency, so respect how much people can take in a single sitting. If time is money, how much should lost people pay to come to your church? The length of your services has to be considered.

DRIVER #4: THE PERMISSIBLE PRESENCE OF GOD

This last one is challenging to articulate. By "permissible," I mean our acknowledgment and welcoming of the Holy Spirit. Of course God doesn't need our permission to do anything. But he also loves his bride and doesn't seem to trespass where she is unwilling or reticent; I'm convinced the Holy Spirit longs to cooperate with the willingness of the Church to submit.

In the realm of the Spirit, this can be fairly subjective. The objective truth is we know that where two or more are gathered, he is in our midst. But the problem is this: for most of us, we need to cultivate that expectation in a child-like way. The simplicity of the prayer, "God, if you don't show up, nothing happens," is rooted in Jesus' statement, *"Apart from me you can do nothing."*[72] That is really less a paralyzing prayer than a prayer of rest and confidence.

I regularly had formerly unchurched people tell me how they felt some sort of peace the first time they walked in. Nearly every other week I would have someone ask me why they wept during worship. I would like to think that it was because of the music or the messages we offered, but frankly, I'm convinced it was simply the presence of God. And that's as it should be. That can't be programmed. But it can be valued...and it should be cherished. There should be a sense of prayerful expectation.

The presence of the Father of compassion is extremely inviting. Are your leaders acknowledging and desiring the reality and presence of God in your services...or have the mechanics of the weekend services overwhelmed this desire? As a one-time worship leader, the most common conversation with my wife on the drive home was, "How did you

---

[72] John 15:5

think the worship went?" and we'd end up talking about the technical things that worked or didn't. But a better question might be, "Did we have a sense of the Spirit's presence during our time together?" Again, this can obviously be subjective, but as leaders, we have to learn to amp up the gift of discernment.

These drivers form the strongest expression of your church's vibe—and your vibe is the strongest reflection of the Water|Servanthood element.

REFLECTION POINTS

Do you have a blurry picture of how servanthood functions in your organization? Do you tend to see servant leadership as a nice, philosophical idea that's untenable in today's hyper-paced world…or worse, makes you appear a weak leader? Are there subtle ways that entitlement has crept into your life-mission…or the team you lead?

What if servanthood is actually the secret sauce for any organization and its long-term effectiveness? A dearth of the Water|Servanthood element invariably opens the door to the cancerous effects of entitlement: me-first attitudes, organizational mistrust, lack of engagement and higher-than-normal turnover rates.

The Jewish Apostle Paul radically defined the new grace-fueled theology of the early Church that has left an indelible impression to this day; his definition of real love[73] is beautifully poetic and revolutionary and read in most weddings in western cultures. But it's when he reluctantly offers his "resume" of suffering that we realize the true power of his leadership. For years, I kept 2 Corinthians 11:23-30 on my laptop's screensaver and would review it when I felt entitle-

---

[73] 1st Corinthians 13

ment hovering over my thoughts or caught myself whining about the pressures of leadership.

For instance, in Paul's incessant missionary travels he...

+ was imprisoned frequently;

+ was flogged several times;

+ received thirty-nine lashes five times;

+ was beaten with rods three times;

+ was the recipient of a stoning that left him for dead;

+ was shipwrecked three times;

+ spent a day and night clinging to a piece of wood in an open sea;

+ was moving constantly city-to-city;

+ was in danger of bandits;

+ was in danger from both his own countrymen, outsiders and phony friends;

+ had gone without sleep, food, and clothes at times;

+ felt the pressures of churchplanting, leading, and maintaining multiple congregations;

+ was self-supporting.

As I mulled over my problems in my comfortable air-conditioned office, Paul's account helped put things in perspective on a regular basis. And it often caused me to mull over two questions, one reflective and one action-oriented:

1. What have I privately sacrificed to advance the purposes of God?

2. What are some ways I could serve the team of people that I directly lead?

While the Water|Servanthood element may be willfully ignored by leaders because of the temptations of power, our next chapter tackles the element that is simply overlooked and typically the least resourced: Air|Imagination.

CHAPTER 5
AIR | IMAGINATION

Christ's love is greater than anyone can ever know, but I pray that you will be able to know that love. Then you can be filled with the fullness of God. With God's power working in us, God can do much, much more than anything we can ask or imagine.

...Often the most important act of executive leadership is *the ability to ask a question that hasn't been asked before*— the ability to inquire, not just dictate or advocate. Unfortunately, most people in executive leadership positions are great at advocacy but poor at inquiry.

Best way—bar none—to stay creative is to manage "hang out." Religiously. *Hang out with weirdos* (on any and all dimensions) rather than "same old, same old" and you automatically win.

The power of imagination is too often overlooked in management and leadership circles and is typically the least active in churches and teams. At a personal level, there may be a physiological reason why we have trouble with innovation and its catalytic instigators: imagination and creativity. According to some neuropsychologists, part of the way our brain functions in order to not burn out is by creating neural pathways so as not to expend energy on what is routine, thereby allowing us to focus on things that need specific attention. But over time, these can become neural ruts. We all have them. And as you might imagine, the older you get, the harder it is to develop new patterns and climb out of old ruts.

Recently, scientists have experimented with replacing the blood of old mice with blood taken from younger mice and discovered in preliminary tests that the old mice subsequently performed faster and smarter in mazes. In certain other experiments, old mice ran twice as long on treadmills than mice that were not given young blood. They have come to believe a particular protein in the blood in young mice produce more neurons, more brain cells…hence, better memory and retention in how they solved problems. Simply put, they got smarter. They literally needed young blood.

Likewise with churches; the older they are, the harder it is to change. As a result, the church grows old along with its members and eventually fades away in its ability to connect with the next generation or culture.

The danger for leaders is believing that imagination is relegated to the exclusive domain of artists and creatives, forgetting that we are all made in the image of a God to whom we are introduced in the opening pages of scripture via an explosion of creativity. We have the same spiritual

DNA, regardless of how artistically-challenged we may consider ourselves. If your best sketches are stick people and the only poetry you recall begins with *"I think that I shall never see...,"* fear not: your true creativity is not limited to doodles and poems.

Ed Catmull, the president of the creative powerhouse Pixar, began his leadership life in front of a computer with a single dream: to somehow create animation with a computer. His boyhood had been shaped by two heroes—Walt Disney and Albert Einstein. Even though he worked his way through Jon Gnagy's *Learn To Draw* art kit, he sadly discovered that he would never reach the talent arc of Disney's animators. So eventually he turned his creativity toward computer science and graphics.

Twenty-five or so years later he would help lead and manage the creative team that developed the industry-changing movie *Toy Story*. But he writes tellingly:

> Everything was going our way, and yet I felt adrift. In fulfilling a goal, I had lost some essential framework. Is this really what I want to do? I began asking myself. The doubts surprised and confused me, and I kept them to myself. . . . There was, in short, plenty to occupy my working hours. But my internal sense of purpose—the thing that had led me to sleep on the floor of the computer lab in graduate school just to get more hours on the mainframe, that kept me awake at night, as a kid, solving puzzles in my head, that fueled my every workday—had gone missing. I'd spent two decades building a train and laying its track. Now, the thought of merely driving it struck me as a far less interesting task. Was making one film after another enough to engage me? I wondered.[74]

---

[74] Catmull, Ed; Wallace, Amy (2014-04-08). *Creativity, Inc.: Overcoming the Unseen Forces That Stand in the Way of True Inspiration* (Kindle Locations 85-87, 91-95). Random House Publishing Group. Kindle Edition.

In other words, Catmull was having a difficult time imagining what part creativity could play in maintaining the operations of a complex company. He would ultimately make a paradigm shift in his thinking: he could use his restless imagination to think about how an organization could develop a "culture of creativity." He began imagining how structures, processes and values could be creatively designed to bring the best out of their employees while satisfying their audience with stories and characters of incredible emotional depth brought to life from zeroes-and-ones (I dare you to watch the four-minute silent montage of Carl and Ellie's entire married life in *"Up"* without getting misty-eyed!).

He could shift his creative juices from graphic programming to thinking innovatively about organizational structures, systems, and culture. Management didn't have to just be about maintenance and metrics; he began to see a much larger picture for his creativity-starved leadership role. He goes on:

> . . . Figuring out how to build a sustainable creative culture—one that didn't just pay lip service to the importance of things like honesty, excellence, communication, originality, and self-assessment but really committed to them, no matter how uncomfortable that became—wasn't a singular assignment. It was a day-in-day-out, full-time job. . . . My hope was to make this culture so vigorous that it would survive when Pixar's founding members were long gone, enabling the company to continue producing original films that made money, yes, but also contributed positively to the world. . . . That was the job I assigned myself—and the one that still animates me to this day.[75]

---

[75] Catmull, Ed; Wallace, Amy (2014-04-08). *Creativity, Inc.: Overcoming the Unseen Forces That Stand in the Way of True Inspiration* (Kindle Location 1077-1086). Random House Publishing Group. Kindle Edition

In my own life, I distinctly remember watching the Beatles on the Ed Sullivan variety show and thinking as a ten-year-old, "That's what I want to do for the rest of my life!" A few years later I was playing in bars most weekends before I could drive. For a number of years I eked out a marginal living as a professional musician, though midstream Jesus overturned my canoe and changed everything, soaking me in his grace. Years later I began my stint with the Vineyard Cincinnati church wearing several different hats, but primarily as a worship leader.

But when my assignment changed to senior pastor, people regularly asked me if I missed leading worship or the "creative arts" aspects of my personality. Instead of feeling conflicted, I discovered that connecting people with Jesus was my primary motivator...and it almost didn't matter what the medium or platform was. And to me, a healthy, grace-infused, missional community had the opportunity to make the biggest impact in a city. Whatever creativity I had was channeled into that vehicle.

What artists often do is begin with the creative question, "What could be?" But leaders who are "Air|Imagination-challenged" will often respond with, "Yes, but artists start with a blank canvas. I have a complex organization that's x-amount-of-years-established with org charts and systems and processes and financial responsibilities and yada yada yada. I don't have a blank canvas!"

But what if you did?

What if you thought differently about those organizational boundaries? In reality, artists have boundaries as well. To start, the size of the canvas. And while their expression of colors seems infinite, they begin with only a few primary ones. They may also have restrictions of time, supplies and their own limited experiences from which their imagination resources. They may also be commissioned and must consider the satisfaction of their benefactor.

One way to think about the leadership "blank canvas" is to begin with the two most basic questions: "What's our business?" and "How are we doing?" Based on that simple "status quo" probe, leaders next have to assess how their current strategy is working and be honest with what's not. That's followed by the obvious question: what will we do differently? That's a huge creative endeavor and the first stab at a corporate blank canvas.

Organizational therapist and author Ichak Adizes writes, "The role of leadership is to lead the necessary change that creates new problems, reintegrate the org to solve those problems, prepare it to be changed again, and have new problems."[76]

Leadership absolutely requires creativity, and as author and international advisor Sir Ken Robinson reminds us,

> Creativity involves putting your imagination to work. In a sense, creativity is applied imagination. Innovation is the process of putting new ideas into practice. Innovation is applied creativity. By definition, innovation is always about introducing something new, or improved, or both and it is usually assumed to be a positive thing.[77]

Imagination begins with asking questions, but before we look at a list of questions to consider, I want to warn you of some barriers that block creativity…and these are often so entrenched in the culture that it's easy to miss them. As you read each one, reflect for a moment on whether it has become embedded in the psyche of your organization.

---

[76] Ichak Adizes; *Managing Corporate Lifecycles* (The Adizes Institute Publishing, 2004), p.9

[77] Robinson, Ken (2011-06-28). *Out of Our Minds: Learning to be Creative* (Kindle Locations 2543-2547). Wiley. Kindle Edition.

IMAGINATION BARRIER #1 FEAR OF CHANGE

Perhaps the biggest barrier to the Air|Imagination element of leadership is the fear of change. We dealt with this issue in chapter three, but it needs to be reiterated here. There is a lot beneath the surface in organizational fear of change, or the leader's personal fear, but every leader must subscribe to a foundational truth that there is no growth without change. And the corollary to that is *there is no change without letting go of the past.*

Growth = Change
...and...
Change = Letting Go of the Past

It's a simple principle, but we can't reach for the *new* without letting go of the *old*...and it's a bit naive to think it won't be painful to some degree. Letting go of anything typically entails a measure of grief, and most of us will avoid grief as much as conflict. Obviously, the greater the sense of loss, the greater the grief and therefore making more important the actual process of grieving. Nevertheless, if we want to grow our ministries in depth, influence, and reach, we will inevitably have to let go of something.

So what do we let go of? Perhaps a better way to think about this is: what should we absolutely *not* let go of?

When we were going through the process of transition from my leadership at Vineyard Cincinnati to the next senior pastor, a consultant posed a revealing question to me: "Dave, what would you say is 'untouchable' for the next lead pastor?" He was obviously trying to expose any assumptions that could prove to be landmines for my successor and particularly how I might interfere if a beloved 'untouchable' was dismissed.

I paused and answered how I *thought* a leader should respond and said, "Absolutely nothing...except for our mission and values." But I was being dishonest. I had a flash of naked fear and immediately began to think of particular programs and ministries that we had birthed in our past and during my tenure that were near and dear to me. As a matter of fact, some had originated during challenging times and at great sacrifice to our people in a particular era.

But deep down I knew they were, in fact, dispensable. Of course I would be hurt at an emotional level, but I knew rationally there were primarily only two non-negotiables: our core mission and values. If those were preserved, I knew the church would be in great shape.

In any organization—and particularly churches—methods and practices can often be confused with values and how the mission is accomplished.

What are we to make of a proper British gentleman who shaved his head except for a braided ponytail, wore sandals and dressed in long silk robes like the people around him? That would be the English missionary, Hudson Taylor, whose mission was to bring the good news of Jesus Christ to China in the mid-1800's. He ended up losing financial support for what others in his homeland considered "compromising the faith." Even more, Britain was actually at war with China at the time; Taylor's efforts would be equivalent to visiting Nazi Germany during the peak of World War II to share Christ with the Allies' sworn enemy. Taylor decided to not turn his converts into "British Christians" but rather "Chinese Christians." He was immensely successful under unimaginable hardships for fifty years.

Taylor's unshakeable value for evangelism—that Jesus came to "seek and save that which was lost"[78]—motivated him to let go of the methodologies and practices of his home culture.

Nowhere is the confusion of practices more evident than when the founder or a well-loved leader transitions out of the organization. The Walt Disney corporation artistically struggled after the death of its highly creative and charismatic founder. Instead of culturalizing Walt's pioneering values, they chose to look backward for decades wrestling through creative decisions with the question, "What would Walt do?" and languished in a creative status quo; the fear of change had overtaken the company psyche. And no organization can take hold of the future while hanging on to the past, especially in the face of our current high-speed cultural changes.

I find the "What Would Jesus Do?"-mantra a bit interesting in this respect. I understand the spirit behind it is connected to Jesus' mission: Jesus would heal, he would love, he would forgive, and so on. But interestingly enough, Jesus seemed to totally mix up his methodologies: for instance, healing the sick might include physical contact, or a simple authoritative command, or spit, or multiple stages due to delayed reactions, or mud...sometimes combined with a poignant teaching point and sometimes in the context of a combative crowd or with a demand for everyone to leave the room.[79] With these varied encounters, it seems more important to capture his values ("God so loved the world," therefore each person is intrinsically valuable) and

---

[78] Luke 19:10

[79] Mark 3:10; Luke 7:1-9; Mark 8:23; Mark 8:25/Luke 17:4; John 9:6; John 11:25-27; Matthew 12:13-14; Matthew 9:25

motivation (indwelling of the Spirit & compassion) and mission ("The son of God appeared for this purpose: to destroy the works of the devil"[80]).

The apostle Paul seemed to flex quite a bit with methods for the sake of his core mission: introducing people to his messiah. He sharply discerned cultural contexts and philosophic/religious sensibilities as evidenced in his powerful message to the Athenian intellectuals in Greece, even respectfully referencing and quoting their own poets and philosophers while challenging their assumptions.[81] It was obvious that Paul was well read and a first-rate thinker. He would later describe his own radical approach to his purpose in life, eschewing what he considered customs for the sake of his personal mission:

> To the Jews I became like a Jew to win the Jews. I myself am not ruled by the law. But to those who are ruled by the law I became like a person who is ruled by the law. I did this to win those who are ruled by the law. To those who are without the law I became like a person who is without the law. I did this to win those people who are without the law. (But really, I am not without God's law—I am ruled by Christ's law.) To those who are weak, I became weak so I could win the weak. I have become all things to all people so I could save some of them in any way possible.[82]

It's easy to gloss over this passage and miss how revolutionary this would have been to his listeners and how easy it could have been misconstrued. But Paul was intentionally pushing the envelope on the tension between method and mission and the easy danger of confusing modes for values.

---

[80] 1 John 3:8b

[81] Acts 17:16-34

[82] 1 Corinthians 9:20-22 (New Century Version)

Paul had become an expert in letting go of the past, even declaring at one point that "*because of him* (Jesus), *I have lost all those things, and now I know they are worthless trash. This allows me to have Christ.*"[83]

Change was the one constant in the early church; they had personally experienced dramatic alterations in their thinking and day-to-day living.

IMAGINATION BARRIER #2: NO PERSONAL TIME INVESTMENT

Let's not kid ourselves: there are natural enemies to the space and time needed to nurture the leader's imagination. So in case I've missed reminding you, let me do so again: leadership is hard. The leaders that we admire—from Moses to Mandela and King David to King Jr.—remind us that putting oneself in front of others only makes for an easy target, from outside forces to your own nagging self-doubts.

Driving an organization often forces us to dive deep into minutiae and the heads-down operational side of leadership. I'm not saying you have to be administratively gifted, but let's get real: operational issues, because they include people and strategies, are virtually unavoidable, no matter how far up the food chain you are. Former USC president and author Stephen Samples writes,

> Virtually all leadership experts, whether they subscribe to traditional or (current) theories, depict leadership as a glamorous and majestic calling. But the contrarian isn't fooled. He knows that effective day-to-day leadership isn't so much about himself, as it is about the men and women he chooses to be his chief lieutenants. He knows that a lot of the things on his own plate will be minutiae and silliness,

---

[83] Philippians 3:8 (New Century Version)

while his lieutenants will get to do the fun and important things.[84]

The element of Air|Imagination is easily choked by the sometimes overwhelming day-to-day routine and thought-consumptive operational-side of leadership, but it is this vital element that is missing in so many churches and organizations. It's the ability to wonder and interact with the question "What if...?"

Carving out an allowance of time to wonder through questions is crucial work for every leader. If you lean toward introversion, it's imperative to regularly schedule alone time to dream about your organization, ministry area, department or family. For instance, I did my best thinking in my car, taking day-long drives by myself, about twice a month, often mulling over a single problem or simply dreaming about what could be. This was not a Moses-complex of "going-up-the-mountain-and-coming-down-with-commandments," but rather a practice for my own sanity and a better way for me to gather my imaginative thoughts since I tended to be a slower, non-verbal processor. As a result, I would take any ideas to our leadership team to process, revamp or question. But the time alone allowed me to mix my imagination with prayer and listening.

Extroverts, you may need to do this with a team of trusted leaders and, if you're an external processor, let them know ahead of time that you're going to throw out a lot of ideas that are not to be taken as mandates. Or it may be a classic brainstorming time with your leadership team, giving them permission to take part in the process while you find this time a creative jumpstart for yourself. Or finding a

---

[84] Stephen Samples; *The Contrarian's Guide to Leadership* (San Francisco, Jossey-Bass, 2002), p.122

trusted consultant that challenges assumptions and probes with questions may be the thing that reframes or refires your creativity.

Regardless, carving out time to engage your imagination in your preferred setting is vital for the people you lead. How much time are you currently giving yourself to dream?

IMAGINATION BARRIER #3: FEAR OF MAKING A MISTAKE

For those of us with perfectionistic personalities, the fear of making a mistake can be debilitating for a leader. But if we're not willing to be wrong, chances are terribly high that we'll never come up with anything creative. Creativity demands the process of elimination. Or as I like to call it, the process of humiliation. Albert Einstein quipped, "Anyone who has never made a mistake, has never tried anything new."

Much has been made of the oft-repeated story of Thomas Edison's light bulb experiments: over 1600 different filament materials were tried and failed until finally finding success with carbonized bamboo—all captured in forty-thousand-plus pages of meticulous notes. Those are a lot of mistakes. But even more telling is Edison's response after experimenting with audio recording. Listening back to the first recording of a human voice—his own, reciting "Mary Had a Little Lamb"—caused him to worry. As he would put it, "I was always afraid of things that worked the first time."[85]

At one point in our history, we were wrestling with how to reach different personality types, particularly those who

---

[85] *Time Machine* magazine, in partnership with the National Museum of American History/Smithsonian Institution, Feb./March 1997, pg. 2, New York, N.Y.

were not attracted to the megachurch model. For those who might be interested in exploring faith in an alternative setting, we launched several microchurches linked to us via video and led by volunteers. We were excited about the possibility of planting churches for the price of a simple, cheap streaming device (though the behind-the-scenes costs turned out to be a significant and expensive overhaul of bringing our outdated video equipment into the world of high definition)! They would function like a house church and be a missional outpost in their own neighborhoods but connected to the resources of a larger church. At the end of a few years, only one survived. For various reasons, we were unsuccessful at making it work and resoundingly failed. There may well be a time when video-resourced mega-church-connected house churches will work, but for us at that point in our history, it didn't.

True innovation absolutely demands failures and false starts because it's simply part of the learning process. Often it's in the failures that our true direction and purpose is discovered. Entrepreneurs know that the company they founded may look and produce things very differently than what they started; for them, it's the initiating and forward-movement aspects that stimulate them.

Wise spiritual leaders have learned that followership is not given because of how perfectly a leader leads, but rather how quickly they own their mistakes and failures. A leader's credibility with their followers is exponentially devalued when he or she shifts blame to others when they're ultimately at fault.

A simple question helps me assess any innovative idea: what's the worst that can happen? Not asking the question is silly. Calculating risk is a part of the creative process, but no idea comes without some risk because invariably, resources will have to shift and priorities reevaluated.

The fear of making a mistake becomes less incapacitating for leaders when they release themselves from thinking they have to be the smartest person at the table. Elemental leaders know that if they've been truly effective at their job, they've hired people who are sharper than themselves, particularly in specialized areas.

But they do have to learn how to be wise. If knowledge is power, wisdom is the ability to apply knowledge and manage power. In a recent study, it was found that leaders who were "generalists" as opposed to "specialists" were more effective in the areas of innovation and creativity. In the corporate world, their firms developed more original patents and invested more in research-and-development. The study showed it wasn't simply that more budget was poured into R&D, but rather generalists improved the productivity and quality in R&D.

Even more interesting was the fact that generalists tend to be less afraid of making mistakes. And because they tended to have worked in a variety of firms and positions, it caused them to think outside the box of a narrow, specialized field.[86]

IMAGINATION BARRIER #4: FEAR OF CHANGING YOUR MIND

Creativity and innovation are often messy and not always linear. One idea that now seems impractical may resurface later and appear revolutionary and absolutely do-able. But often leaders don't want to be viewed as weak because of flip-flopping on a particular initiative, or worse, not knowing what she is doing. Personally, I'm not sure I would ever

---

[86] http://www.ideasforleaders.com/ideas/generalist-ceos-not-specialists-spur-innovation

want to follow someone who can't, or will not, change their mind, especially in our high-speed world of transition and change.

Elemental leaders know that being right is not nearly as important as the right solution. And *un*learning is just as critical as learning when dealing with creative solutions and innovation.

IMAGINATION BARRIER #5: A CULTURE OF DISTRUST

In biology, culture is what grows in the petri dish when the right chemical pool is present. But the type of culture is dependent on which growth medium is used. In other words, you shape the culture by the conditions you establish. Shaping leadership and staff culture is one of the primary jobs of a leader. Typically, the best creativity that can happen in a team context is one where trust has been built and nurtured.

Conversely, asking future-thinking questions in a culture of distrust or fear will yield zero results. Presenting creative ideas in that kind of an atmosphere raises the "risk bar" to heights only the most self-secure or even arrogant personalities can hurdle and will severely limit the input of introverts and creatives who connect personal worth with their creativity. Sharing an imaginative thought is a risk for most people: none of us want to look stupid. Nurturing an atmosphere of trust is vital if you want the richest creativity.

In a trust-laden culture, new ideas and innovations can be shaped, pushed back on, clarified, questioned, and reworked to be made even better, but only if the originator of the idea feels safe and affirmed in who they are and their place in the organization. Ken Robinson reminds us of the power of collective imagination in a "creative-safe" environment and the nurturing role the leader has:

> Being a creative leader means ensuring that everyone in the organization is playing to their creative strengths and feels that their contribution is valued as part of the overall performance of the organization.[87]

Organizations with a culture of trust tend to encourage *intra*preneurship, creating an entrepreneurial culture *inside* the company, launching new ideas and ministries within the parameters of the vision and values. That means the organization has to give some space for trying things that may or may not succeed or pay off in the typical ways. For instance, a vital ministry for special needs children was developed in our family ministries area simply because some key volunteers had personal experience with the need and were given permission to explore what it could look like, eventually turning into a successful ministry called BridgeBuilders.

In some ways, BridgeBuilders led to another initiative and an example of intrapreneurship. One of our staff had been a Christian kid growing up, a "good girl," active and well-liked. In high school, Harmony contracted a viral disease and ended up having nearly twenty surgeries to remove tumors in her neck, missing over two-hundred days of school. At one point, the nerves in her face stopped working correctly and she found herself slurring her words, drooling in a stroke-like condition. Imagine your impressionable high school years and the unique cruelty of school kids. Because she missed so much school, she was put in what was called the "slow classes" back then. During that

---

[87] Robinson, Ken (2011-06-28). *Out of Our Minds: Learning to be Creative* (Kindle Location 3884). Wiley. Kindle Edition.

experience, she felt as though God whispered to her, "Don't forget this time."

Harmony eventually recovered, but years later what she wanted to do at the Vineyard was throw a free party for adults with special needs, particularly a prom, which is a serious event for high school kids in America: a big, final dance when they graduate. This party would be designed especially for special needs adults who more-than-likely were never invited to a prom. She mobilized hundreds of volunteers and created the first one that drew over eight-hundred special needs adults. We repeated it for several years.

There were calculated risks with the prom, including significant safety issues, and the potential of being a mistake in terms of resources and return. It wasn't. Within a culture of trust, intrapreneurship can yield surprising results and release leaders into substantial ministries.

IMAGINATION BARRIER #6: PROBLEM-AVOIDANCE

Decades ago, becoming a *learning organization* was a common call-to-action in organizational development circles.[88] That is, it was imperative to develop a culture of continual improvement individually and corporately by various disciplines, such as creating systems and structures for sharing and codifying best practices when there is a clear vision and common ownership. It was as much about learning *how* we learn together. This becomes even more critical in our era of rapidly shifting mores and technologies. Change and learning should be inextricable.

For some of the churches I've encountered, it's change or die.

---

[88] Peter Senge's "The Fifth Discipline" was an early promoter of the learning organization

Learning organizations hope to avoid chronic or repeating problems. But what really pushes the learning organization are problems themselves, whether internal or external. The truth is: innovation and its creative force—imagination—is driven by problems.

Problems create conflict and conflict, within reason, is critical. It's out of conflict that things grow; for instance, every season can't be sunny summer days, otherwise, all living things would dry up and die. Grey rainy days are necessary.

But what is vital is how we view conflict and how we manage it. Or to put it another way, you learned to tie your shoes because it wasn't optimal to ask mom or dad to tie them every time they came undone. Plus, individuation was a necessary part of growing up and the problem of a hovering parent wasn't cool.

My preferred operational mode is harmony; I don't function well in high-conflict cultures. Conflict sucks the energy out of me. But trying to maintain a "conflict-free" zone is unhealthy, not to mention impossible. We don't live in a virus-free world. Rainstorms come and go. Shoestrings break.

If you're a pastor, you know and experience this deeply: conflict goes with the territory! But how you view it, and the innovation it can spur, is important. The job of leadership is to help others see how conflict can be healthy in order for the best solutions to be discovered, and at the very least, impossible to avoid.

Some of the best and most energizing moments can be when you as a leader assemble your team, your elders, your board or key volunteers to tackle an issue. If we've taken the time to create and reinforce a supportive learning environment, these can be shining moments for our church or organization and bring out our creative best.

In his landmark book *Corporate Lifecycles: How Organizations Grow and Die and What to Do about It,* Dr. Ichak Adizes laid out organizations' life stages on a Bell curve.

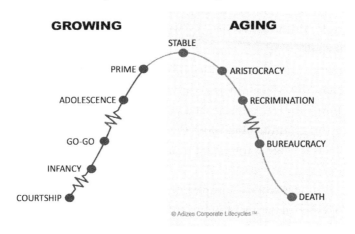

© Adizes Corporate Lifecycles ™

According to Adizes, every stage has unique problems that must be solved. That's normal; if you're not having problems, you're dead.

When a typical problem happens within a particular life cycle, we apply energy to solve it and hopefully put in place what can be preventive the next time. A problem is considered abnormal if it occurs in the wrong lifecycle, in the wrong timing, like "mumps, say, in middle age, or prostate trouble in adolescence"[89], as Adizes explains. In order to understand whether a problem is abnormal or not, a leader has to identify where they are on the Bell curve as it relates to the Prime stage—whether moving forward toward it or trying to return to it. Research lead Adizes to this discovery:

---

[89] Inc. Magazine; October 1, 1996; Adizes, Ichak; The 10 Stages of Corporate Life Cycles

the organization has a critical need to stay in a state of Prime and, interestingly enough, not settle in Stable. Abnormal and chronic problems will cause an organization to stall, burn out, or even rush through later lifecycles that set up an early death if not dealt with appropriately, even when everything seems to be charting up-and-to-the-right. In his study, Prime is that delicate balance between organizational flexibility and self-control, or creativity and discipline. And in my mind, that's a leadership responsibility based on good data, sharp teammates, and some intuitive smarts. For church leaders, add the vital need to keep your prophetic ear to the ground. One more thing to note: an organization's lifecycle stage is unrelated to its size, assets or chronological age.

Prime is when a complex organization begins to get its act together in terms of being truly driven by its values, has a true system of checks and balances—or accountability—with a functioning government, is creating healthy integrated departments—or in our case, ministries—that are interdependent, and knows which activities it should be spending its resources on. In Prime, there is always a tension between being flexible and entrepreneurial and having self-control in what it spends its time, the energy of its people and their resources on. In Prime, we know what to do and what not to do...why and why not... how and how not to do it. Adizes states it like this:

> A prime organization is not subject to the shifting wishes of a single person. It is guided and led by a message—a vision of its reason for being. The people in the organization believe that what they are doing is important.[90]

[90] Ichak Adizes; *Managing Corporate Lifecycles* (The Adizes Institute Publishing, 2004), p.97

With apologies to Adizes, let me reinterpret his lifecycle stages for church leaders:

+ In the *Courtship* phase, a leader entertains ideas of churchplanting and imagines what effect they could have in a particular community. They have been infused with a "let's go change the world" attitude.

+ In *Infancy*, the rubber meets the road: dreams and plans are now connected to results. The churchplanter is networking and meeting with ridiculous amounts of people. Systems and processes aren't important—survival is. The churchplanter is working insane hours and doing everything themselves. Any forward movement is dependent on them.

+ *Go-Go* is all about fast growth; numbers are exploding, lives are being transformed, people are excited about the mission. When this is happening, the churchplanter has morphed into the lead pastor and can begin to feel bulletproof and secretly arrogant. Even though everyone on the team is wearing multiple hats, the lead pastor is still making all the decisions.

+ With the *Adolescence* stage, the lead pastor may hire an executive pastor but will find it hard to let go of any decision-making. An "old-timers" versus "new people" culture (perhaps surrounding the executive pastor) creates internal conflicts and the vision gets blurry. So much time can be spent dealing with internal issues that the church loses sight of whom it is to serve.

+ In *Prime*, the church rediscovers its soul, vision is recovered, and it nurtures the balance between creativity/innovation/flexibility and organizational discipline and self-control. The church has a renewed outward-focus, serving others and Jesus with healthy gusto. New ministries and new churches are birthed that may create more opportunities for other lifecycles and hiving off.

+ The *Stability* phase marks a dangerous turn for the church: it's still healthy but losing some of its edge and energy. New ideas aren't as easily accepted and excitement about innovation has waned. Financial controls are more pronounced and affecting creativity for future impact.

+ With *Aristocracy* comes organizational entitlement. The church no longer talks about why it does certain things or even what it does, but *how* it does it becomes the focal point. Respectability reigns and the church is relying on its past to move them forward. Image becomes critical. In corporations, acquisition becomes more important than incubation. What that means in churches is that people transfer into the church while church planting and new ministries are lost in the shuffle.

+ The *Recrimination* stage is all about blame and finger pointing. The church is declining, elders dig in and protect power, new pastors float in and out, and ministries and staff are reduced because of finances. Backstabbing, gossip and infighting rule the day.

+ *Bureaucracy* is the last gasp. Policies and procedures reign. The church may have even died before getting to this stage. The church has lost any prophetic voice and is irrelevant to the community.

+ And finally, *Death*. It might have been slow or sudden, but there's no reason to continue. The church building and assets are sold.

Ultimately, chronic problems in any organization will stem from a leadership issue somewhere. In the history of leadership in the Old Testament, the momentum and mission-fulfillment of Israel ebbed and flowed based on a king's leadership. Their sad history is laid out warts-and-all…and it isn't pretty.

BEGIN ASKING QUESTIONS

Leaders with a bent toward the Air|Imagination element have a natural curiosity regarding what could be, often questioning the status quo with *"What if…"*-style questions. They tend to have an entrepreneurial bent or an internal research-and-development engine that purrs with ideas and wonderments, typically toying with questions regarding effectiveness, whether involving mission, structures, personnel, methodologies, priorities or culture. In his book *How the Mighty Fall: And Why Some Companies Never Give In*, Jim Collins recalls an invaluable lesson his mentor, Bill Lazier, taught him: don't try to come up with the right answers; focus on coming up with good questions.[91]

All leaders must learn to cultivate the quality of asking questions in their organization. It breathes life into teams. It can be imaginative, such as:

+ If you quit and then were hired as the new lead pastor, what would you change?

+ What if you ruthlessly evaluated and innovated your evangelism methods?

+ What if people could find and connect to a small group in a Match.com-style web-based approach?

+ What if once a year everyone in the church did a spiritual gifts assessment instead of having a regular service?

+ How would your key leaders describe your church/organizational culture in one-word descriptions?

[91] Jim Collins; *How the Mighty Fall: And Why Some Companies Never Give In* (New York, HarperCollins, 2011), p.2

+ What would your staff or key volunteers say is the primary purpose of your weekend services?

+ If you changed the name of your church, what could it be?

+ What is the greatest felt-need in your community?

+ What if you told your city council that your church would totally clean up after the next street festival?

+ What if thirty churches in your city canceled their weekend services one weekend, and instead met together in a large central location for worship, took up an offering and gave it to an inner-city school for needed resources? How might that change the way people in your city view Christians?

+ What language in your church has lost its meaning?

+ What if one weekend you gave all the offering to another organization in your city?

+ How might you get every small group to "own" a particular mission or ministry?

+ What would cause the biggest "head-tilt" from people outside the church and cause them to re-question their stereotyped assumptions about Christianity?

+ If you could recreate the atmosphere of your church, what would it feel like?

+ Which of the four elements need to be amped up in your current situation?

+ What if you offered a "free yard sale" and asked your church members to donate gently used stuff to give away?

+ What would a holistic approach to meeting people's needs look like?

+ What if each year your staff identified one 20-something leader that could potentially plant a church…and began to intentionally mentor them toward that?

+ What if you identified two specific ways you could serve the leaders who follow you?

+ What if you filled your lobbies with empty boxes with a grocery list attached to feed a family of four and had your members take one home, collect the goods and give them away at Thanksgiving?

+ What would help create some entrepreneurial ministry and R&D in your church?—in other words, who needs permission?

...and the questions can go on. If the Air|Imagination element is not your strongest inclination, these types of questions may feel overwhelming and frustrating, but a leader with this dominant element will actually find them energizing.

REFLECTION POINTS

As mentioned earlier, the Air|Imagination element is often overlooked in leadership development material in the same way that research-and-development is usually the first budget item to get cut during lean times. But don't let that stop you: my personal experience is that creative thinking is often best expressed when resources are thin, forcing more innovative ways to attack problems or promote growth.

Regardless, carve out some time to reflect on how your organization is nurturing its creative juices or, conversely, how subliminal or subconscious forces are hindering any entrepreneurial or intrapreneurial thinking. Are you overdue for some innovative ways to further your mission and vision or realigning resources to achieve greater impact?

When was the last Big Idea that caused your mission to leap forward? Is it time for a new one?

CHAPTER 6
DISCOVERING YOUR ELEMENT

When Jesus saw Nathanael approaching, he said of him,
"Here is a true Israelite, in whom there is nothing false."
"How do you know me?" Nathanael asked.

~JOHN 1:47-48a

Know thyself.

~(ATTRIBUTED TO) HERACLITUS, SOCRATES, PLATO,
AESCHYLUS...OR ANY OTHER GREEK SAGE

T he following *Elemental Leader Personal Assessment*™ is designed to determine which element you naturally lean into. You can fill it in here or, better yet, online at *www.elementalinventory.com/assessments*. Either way, you'll need to fill in your answers online to determine your scores—the process is free. As you read each question, ask yourself, "Do I really...?" In other words, be brutally honest. After all, there are no right or wrong answers.

The survey is not intended to measure your "strengths and weaknesses," but rather to identify your natural leadership style and to see how the four elements are balanced within it. While we all have distinct gifts, talents, and personalities, the most effective leaders will be self-aware and will surround themselves with others who together create a well-balanced team.

The following sixty questions take the form of statements about your own priorities and leadership style. For each, indicate whether that statement is true of you as you perceive yourself using a five-point scale: strongly disagree; disagree; neutral (or not sure how to answer); agree; strongly agree. For this survey, first impressions may be more helpful than well-considered answers, so feel free to go with your first impulse.

Elemental Leader Personal Assessment ™

(check one) □*strongly disagree*   □*disagree*   □*neutral*   □*agree*   □*strongly agree*

1. I prefer to start projects rather than finish them.

   □*strongly disagree*   □*disagree*   □*neutral*   □*agree*   □*strongly agree*

2. I value predictable results over originality.

   □*strongly disagree*   □*disagree*   □*neutral*   □*agree*   □*strongly agree*

3. I prefer to plan and/or serve in events that connect to people outside our church.

   □*strongly disagree*   □*disagree*   □*neutral*   □*agree*   □*strongly agree*

4. I generally prefer innovative solutions over traditional approaches even if the old way seems to promise the results I want.

   □*strongly disagree*   □*disagree*   □*neutral*   □*agree*   □*strongly agree*

5. Serving the needs of my team members is generally more important to me than meeting goals.

   □*strongly disagree*   □*disagree*   □*neutral*   □*agree*   □*strongly agree*

6. I generally rely on policy and procedures as my guides to negotiating difficult situations rather than considerations about the situations and feelings of individuals.

   □*strongly disagree*   □*disagree*   □*neutral*   □*agree*   □*strongly agree*

7. Innovation is more important to me than building consensus.

   □*strongly disagree*   □*disagree*   □*neutral*   □*agree*   □*strongly agree*

8. Stability is more important than accomplishment.

    ☐*strongly disagree* ☐*disagree* ☐*neutral* ☐*agree* ☐*strongly agree*

9. Whenever I read communication from our church or website, I typically find myself asking how someone outside our church might interpret what we are saying.

    ☐*strongly disagree* ☐*disagree* ☐*neutral* ☐*agree* ☐*strongly agree*

10. Change is more important to long-term success than stability.

    ☐*strongly disagree* ☐*disagree* ☐*neutral* ☐*agree* ☐*strongly agree*

11. I often wonder how people outside our church would respond to what we are saying or doing.

    ☐*strongly disagree* ☐*disagree* ☐*neutral* ☐*agree* ☐*strongly agree*

12. I typically view problems as opportunities.

    ☐*strongly disagree* ☐*disagree* ☐*neutral* ☐*agree* ☐*strongly agree*

13. In general, my first impulse is to think more about ideas and possibilities than about their impact on individuals.

    ☐*strongly disagree* ☐*disagree* ☐*neutral* ☐*agree* ☐*strongly agree*

14. Obstacles tend to energize me rather than discourage me.

    ☐*strongly disagree* ☐*disagree* ☐*neutral* ☐*agree* ☐*strongly agree*

15. Staying true to my personal values is more important to me than achieving goals.

    ☐*strongly disagree* ☐*disagree* ☐*neutral* ☐*agree* ☐*strongly agree*

16. People would tend to perceive me as steady and reliable rather than as a mover and shaker.

    ☐*strongly disagree* ☐*disagree* ☐*neutral* ☐*agree* ☐*strongly agree*

17. I'm better at creating than encouraging.

    □*strongly disagree* □*disagree* □*neutral* □*agree* □*strongly agree*

18. I regularly mention the names of people on my team when I write or talk about what we are doing.

    □*strongly disagree* □*disagree* □*neutral* □*agree* □*strongly agree*

19. Budgetary and other resource considerations are the most important factors in the early stages of my planning process.

    □*strongly disagree* □*disagree* □*neutral* □*agree* □*strongly agree*

20. In meetings, I tend to focus on "What?" and "When?" questions more than "Why?" and "How?"

    □*strongly disagree* □*disagree* □*neutral* □*agree* □*strongly agree*

21. When someone isn't performing well, my first impulse is to help her/him improve rather than looking for a replacement.

    □*strongly disagree* □*disagree* □*neutral* □*agree* □*strongly agree*

22. Fulfilling our mission is generally more important to me than meeting the needs of my team members.

    □*strongly disagree* □*disagree* □*neutral* □*agree* □*strongly agree*

23. In considering an opportunity, I generally first analyze whether we have the resources to succeed.

    □*strongly disagree* □*disagree* □*neutral* □*agree* □*strongly agree*

24. People would say that I do the things I say are important.

    □*strongly disagree* □*disagree* □*neutral* □*agree* □*strongly agree*

25. When someone exhibits a poor attitude or doesn't seem capable, my first impulse is to look for a replacement rather than helping her/him improve.

    □*strongly disagree* □*disagree* □*neutral* □*agree* □*strongly agree*

26. I value creativity over predictable outcomes.

    □*strongly disagree* □*disagree* □*neutral* □*agree* □*strongly agree*

27. In general, my first impulse is to think more about how new ideas and possibilities might impact my team members than about whether we should implement them.

    □*strongly disagree* □*disagree* □*neutral* □*agree* □*strongly agree*

28. I enjoy working with creative people, even though they might be high maintenance.

    □*strongly disagree* □*disagree* □*neutral* □*agree* □*strongly agree*

29. I energize others around me to act.

    □*strongly disagree* □*disagree* □*neutral* □*agree* □*strongly agree*

30. I rely heavily on intuition in goal-setting and decision-making processes.

    □*strongly disagree* □*disagree* □*neutral* □*agree* □*strongly agree*

31. I look for ways to help my team members grow and develop.

    □*strongly disagree* □*disagree* □*neutral* □*agree* □*strongly agree*

32. I often think about ways we could revise programs or processes with a view to making it easier for new people to become involved.

    □*strongly disagree* □*disagree* □*neutral* □*agree* □*strongly agree*

33. I regularly ask, "What if we…?"

□strongly disagree   □disagree   □neutral   □agree   □strongly agree

34. Building and maintaining systems of accountability is important to me.

□strongly disagree   □disagree   □neutral   □agree   □strongly agree

35. When considering possibilities or evaluating what I am doing, I frequently ask myself how an activity aligns with our mission statement.

□strongly disagree   □disagree   □neutral   □agree   □strongly agree

36. Achievement is more important than stability.

□strongly disagree   □disagree   □neutral   □agree   □strongly agree

37. I'm better at building into people than coming up with new ideas.

□strongly disagree   □disagree   □neutral   □agree   □strongly agree

38. People would say that I inspire them to try things they otherwise might not.

□strongly disagree   □disagree   □neutral   □agree   □strongly agree

39. I often challenge people to think differently.

□strongly disagree   □disagree   □neutral   □agree   □strongly agree

40. I frequently talk about things that excite me.

□strongly disagree   □disagree   □neutral   □agree   □strongly agree

41. I am more energized by the thought of attracting new people to our church than by efforts to retain the people we already have.

□strongly disagree   □disagree   □neutral   □agree   □strongly agree

42. Stability is more important to long-term success than change.

□strongly disagree □disagree □neutral □agree □strongly agree

43. Building consensus is more important to me than innovation.

□strongly disagree □disagree □neutral □agree □strongly agree

44. I prefer to see projects through to the finish rather than starting new ones.

□strongly disagree □disagree □neutral □agree □strongly agree

45. People would describe me as an "all or nothing" person.

□strongly disagree □disagree □neutral □agree □strongly agree

46. I readily make exceptions to fixed policies and procedures to address the unique needs and feelings of individuals.

□strongly disagree □disagree □neutral □agree □strongly agree

47. Whenever I read a communication from our church or our website, I am generally more concerned that we have communicated clearly to our members than with how visitors or newer people might respond.

□strongly disagree □disagree □neutral □agree □strongly agree

48. When I encounter obstacles, I tend to reconsider my objectives and attempt to come up with new goals and plans.

□strongly disagree □disagree □neutral □agree □strongly agree

49. I am willing to set my values aside to achieve an important objective.

□strongly disagree □disagree □neutral □agree □strongly agree

50. In the early stages of my planning process, I focus primarily on human factors: how people might react, how to anticipate and overcome objections, communications strategies, etc.

□*strongly disagree* □*disagree* □*neutral* □*agree* □*strongly agree*

51. In meetings, I tend to ask "Why not?" and "Could we?" more than "By when?" and "Can we be sure this will meet our goals?"

□*strongly disagree* □*disagree* □*neutral* □*agree* □*strongly agree*

52. People often describe me as enthusiastic.

□*strongly disagree* □*disagree* □*neutral* □*agree* □*strongly agree*

53. I don't care much whether a model or method is new, old, innovative, or conventional, so long as it produces the desired results.

□*strongly disagree* □*disagree* □*neutral* □*agree* □*strongly agree*

54. People who seek my advice would generally say that I provide a mature perspective.

□*strongly disagree* □*disagree* □*neutral* □*agree* □*strongly agree*

55. People would describe my approach to life and work as "balanced."

□*strongly disagree* □*disagree* □*neutral* □*agree* □*strongly agree*

56. I seek data on emerging cultural trends and projected future developments when thinking about program possibilities.

□*strongly disagree* □*disagree* □*neutral* □*agree* □*strongly agree*

57. I value input from individuals who do not agree with the ways we do things.

□strongly disagree   □disagree   □neutral   □agree   □strongly agree

58. While I care about people, I make a conscious effort not to allow personal considerations to stop me from hitting a target.

□strongly disagree   □disagree   □neutral   □agree   □strongly agree

59. People would tend to perceive me as a "change agent" rather than as a "stabilizer."

□strongly disagree   □disagree   □neutral   □agree   □strongly agree

60. It's difficult for me to put aside considerations of how decisions might impact individuals, even when a proposed course of action is very likely to produce results that support a goal.

□strongly disagree   □disagree   □neutral   □agree   □strongly agree

SCORING:

Enter your answers in the personal assessment survey at *www.elementalinventory.com/assessements.* Fill in your scores here:

_____ (Earth|Integrity)
_____ (Fire|Passion)
_____ (Water|Servanthood)
_____ (Air|Imagination)

Your highest total is your dominant elemental leadership trait. Typically, you'll assess with 2-3 similarly scored elements and one that is obviously lower, which is often your blind spot when it comes situational leadership.

No leader can perpetually function in all four elements nor is it necessary to amplify all the elements all the time. Determining which element needs to be focused on in your current context is what we'll tap into in the next section.

But most leaders naturally lean more into one or two than the others. That's normal. At certain points, though, a leader's team or organization will need an infusion of one of the elements, and it may be missed if the leader's personality is weighted heavily toward a different element. As the popular maxim goes: if all you have is a hammer, everything looks like a nail.

Let's look at some leaders with hyperbolized elements.

Janelle

Everyone respects and trusts Janelle. In her role as executive director of the Madison House—a transition home for adults with recovery issues—Janelle has developed healthy processes and policies for dealing with difficult interpersonal concerns. She is crystal clear regarding the purpose of the Madison House and a stickler for how things get done, often getting personally involved. Her staff has the highest respect for her, even though some may feel a bit micromanaged from time-to-time.

Janelle has grown over the last few years in understanding how uniquely non-profits function since she left a lucrative corporate executive role, even though she volunteered one night a week at Madison for nearly six years prior to that. She believes that the primary way to maintain effectiveness is by paying attention to systems. Her former boss schooled her in MBWA—Management By Wandering Around[92]—in

---

[92] Peters & Waterman; *In Search of Excellence: Lessons From America's Best-Run Companies,* (New York: Harper Business/HarperCollins; 1982)

order to know who's doing what and why. Janelle is recognized by her steadiness and reliability; she firmly believes the buck stops with her and that she's accountable for building a solid organization. To her, that goal is far more rewarding than any personal gain or recognition.

Although not necessarily seen as a charismatic leader in the natural sense, Janelle jokes easily about her introversion in fun, self-deprecating ways. But her pursuit of organizational health has dismantled "silos" in her organization and created seamless processes to ensure the mission of the Madison House is accomplished. And though she is not seen as an impassioned personality or necessarily creative, people follow her because of her steadfastness and her strong work ethic.

Janelle is primarily grounded in the Earth|Integrity element.

Chad

Chad is a mercurial leader…sometimes up and down, compelling and catalytic, driven and demanding. His staff and volunteers have learned to deal with his frustrations and, behind the scenes, laugh at his idiosyncrasies because they love him and frankly he makes things happen. They love the mission he's given the church and his laser-focus on it. The people around him are tired but feel that their energies have been well spent.

Chad's timing and tone are not always ideal when he's pointing out things that need to change, but people around him chalk it up to passion. He often speaks his mind before his thoughts are fully fleshed out, and though some personalities get flustered with his style, he dismisses it to oversensitivity on their part. Chad networks easily and quickly and may be unfairly stereotyped as having relationships that are wide and an inch deep, but he sees his responsibility to accomplishing the mission as paramount. He often thrives on conflict and contrarian viewpoints that seem to energize his passion for innovation and accomplishment.

While this is admittedly oversimplified, Chad is a classic Fire|Passion leader. This is not to imply that he doesn't appreciate or practice the other elements, but his go-to mode is an obvious fervor for the mission and ministry. He may embrace servanthood and appreciate the necessary systems and processes by which mission is accomplished, but it's not where his energy taps into or builds from.

Damon

During a long, intense strategic planning meeting, Damon recognized that the conversation bogged down and energy was flagging. As lead pastor, he called for a fifteen-minute break and stepped out of the room. After bathroom breaks, email checks, and some stretch walking, the leadership team returned to the room to find a take-out carton of specialty coffee and a mix of munchies on the table. The team made some jokes about it then Damon suggested they take time to do a simple personal check in. The team relaxed as each one mentioned some individual challenges in their family or some new positive changes with their kids or some self-disclosing but funny personal mishap. They felt free enough to do that because Damon had personally been vulnerable in past settings and one-on-one meetings. After decompression, the team dug back into some organizational problem-solving that had stalled before the break. With renewed energy, their culture of high-level trust enabled them to honestly and truthfully poke below the surface within their own areas of ministry.

Critics might observe that Damon would do well to give more attention to performance benchmarks and tangible results, but would also readily state that he places great emphasis on the human dimension. Even people who question his decisions feel affirmed by him and would never doubt that he cares. Damon is often present at key moments in his team member's lives: visiting the hospital when they or a family member is sick, sending a card of congratulations for a birth in the family, or attending a daughter's high school graduation. People do not follow Damon because he excels in articulating a vision or managing systems, but rather because they trust him.

Damon easily swims in the Water|Servanthood element, convinced that love expressed through serving others in the workplace is a power to be reckoned with…and in the end, breeds long-term productivity.

Dara

Dara leads with a creative edge that sometimes causes others to shake their heads in amazement at what she can come up. Thriving in an atmosphere of questions and wonderments, and driving people to think deeply about why they do what they do, her leadership brings a freshness to problem-solving. But it goes beyond that, launching entrepreneurial thinking and an expansive slant to mission. Dara is quick to experiment with current structures and systems. The way she communicates a vision of what "could be" is authentically inspirational and challenging. Like a houseflipper who sees the hidden potential of a blighted property, Dara views her organization as a field of possibilities as she paints compelling pictures of the future. If her ideas are sometimes unrealistic, they are never lacking in imagination.

Dara is undaunted by limited resources and flourishes in an environment of possibility-thinking. People follow her because she's mentally stimulating and seemingly unafraid of making mistakes. She's quick to own up to failures while insisting they're necessary in order to develop a fearless culture of achievement. Critics say she sometimes takes a "flavor of the month" approach but regularly use the word "brilliant" when describing her. They might observe that it wouldn't hurt if she gave more thought to the realities of limited resources, and sometimes wonder "how she thinks all this will get done." Without meaning to discourage her, they kindly advise her to "slow down," which Dara takes as evidence that things are moving along just fine.

Dara doesn't eschew servanthood or integrity, but clearly the Air|Imagination element is her modus operandi. Passion is often used as a tool to further her creative ideas with others, but it typically serves to support her Air-element strength. She can move too quickly for some on her team and those who want to test an idea first, but her imagination is definitely the catalyst for making things happen. Status quo and routine are her enemies.

Although these people are stereotyped, are there one or two that you most identify yourself with? I've observed that many leaders function fairly well in several elements, but tend to favor one or two. Often during a crisis or a nagging less-than-stellar corporate performance, elemental leaders may default to amping up their naturally strongest and dominant element to detrimental effect.

For instance, when a church has drifted into a stable bureaucracy and hasn't launched a creative, entrepreneurial outreach or mission in several years, Janelle (Earth|Integrity) may sense something is missing and invest time in shifting departments, wrestling with org charts or researching current bylaws with the board, working hard to make internal changes. While all those things are important, a larger issue is at stake at this point. And Damon (Water|Servanthood) might get buried in the development of a consensus-building and affiliative processes to making his teams and meetings more effective and cohesive as he recognizes this drift.

But the real problem is likely the loss of a hill to take. And not just clarity regarding their mission, but the need for something outside of themselves to missionally accomplish together. The flurry of activity in which Janelle and Damon are engaged may easily be confused with the real work that needs to be done.

Or perhaps the most current issue is that the church has way too many irons in the fire and resources are spread thin as they try to accomplish way too much in often competing ministries. There is no clear focus since everything is "important." Volunteers are constantly coming up with new ideas to meet the plethora of perceived needs in the community but fight to get their particular interest—and needs—announced each Sunday. Chad's Fire|Passion approach is simple: he excitedly picks his personal favorite initiatives that people have launched and ignores others, sometimes leading to confusion among volunteers and ministry directors. His own leadership team often asks, "What would Chad do?" Determining what to stop doing is difficult for them.

For Dara and her Air|Imagination leanings, the preceding problem of unbridled entrepreneurialism would leave her unfazed. She might view it with a "survival of the fittest" approach…simply see what sticks. But instead, the church will subliminally develop its own criteria for what's effective and important. And with too many cooks in the kitchen, it's unclear who's really the head chef and eventually vision will suffer.

ELEMENTAL LEADERSHIP TEAMS

Developing a leadership team that recognizes the importance of the four elements and becomes adept at discerning when one of them is flagging or, conversely, has received too much attention in the organization, is critical. This is where the simplicity of the four elements, the assessment and having a common language is helpful.

For instance, one church I was familiar with had plateaued in terms of growth, health, and frankly, energy and momentum. This can be a complex problem and good coaches will look at everything like leadership competencies, communication skills, systems, inter-relational issues, facility constraints, team dynamics, environments, and so on. Having skilled outsiders suggest fresh perspectives from time-to-time is vital; it's too easy for leaders to become myopic.

But after becoming familiar with the four elements, the leadership team realized that the Fire|Passion element had long flamed out. It had been years since they launched anything new or fresh and a very long time since they challenged their people in a big way. Remember the Shushwap story from Chapter 5? Similarly, this church had settled into predictable routines that had caused a subtle organizational boredom and was in dire need of stretching beyond their comfort zones.

This simple discovery also led to a spirited conversation about the Air|Imagination element…and the fact that they really didn't have anyone in their leadership circle who was entrepreneurial in ministry opportunities. Their senior pastor felt some "leadership discomfort" at this point—obviously, he knew where the buck stopped and felt responsible. But because they had developed a healthy Water| Servanthood culture, he was secure in who he was.

Although the conversation would occasionally wander off on rabbit trails, they eventually identified an imagination barrier in their leadership and the life of the church they all loved: a fear of change. Because they had settled into a comfortable stability, they somehow missed the voice of the Holy Spirit who draws us into the creative tension between invitation and challenge.

In a subsequent meeting, they developed a simple strategy that included a retreat with guided prayer to help them hear from God, along with spending part of their time with a facilitator with an entrepreneurial background to fire up their neurons. Their senior pastor also realized that the cloistered administrative work of the church had sucked out some of his passion for their original outward-focused mission. His team developed a plan to off-load the majority of that work from his schedule and allow for some imaginative "think-time" in his week.

While it would be ideal to have each element spearheaded by a person on the executive leadership team, there at least has to be a clear pathway and strategy to catalyze a particular element that's missing. But more important is the need to assess which element your organization needs to energize...or throttle.

Which brings us to the next chapter.

CHAPTER 7
ASSESSING YOUR CHURCH

*From the tribe of Issachar, there were two-hundred leaders of
the tribe with their relatives. All these men understood the
signs of the times and knew the best course for Israel to take.*

~1 CHRONICLES 12:32
(NEW LIVING TRANSLATION, SECOND EDITION)

The primary objective for any leader is to discern what the "best course" is for the people they lead. In other words: what needs to be done today in order to complete the mission tomorrow? Elemental leaders are consumed with determining what is needed to keep their church healthy, effective and moving forward. But that also implies they have a high degree of organizational "self-awareness."

At a practical level, the way leaders determine what is organizationally needed is by data (actual metrics and measurements) or by intuition (which can be subjective and anecdotally-driven, but it's why good leaders stay engaged with the people they lead, as in Janelle's MBWA—Management By Wandering Around—in chapter 6). Spiritual leaders recognize a critical third way: insight from the Holy Spirit (for instance, Paul's vision that diverted a mission trip to Northern Greece[93]). This third way needs to be measured and balanced as carefully as we would intuition; the New Testament implies that it's tested and confirmed by other mature leaders in your community.

By periodically probing your leadership team—and your own heart—through a series of questions, you may be surprised at what you uncover…and what you may have already known in your leadership gut.

THE BIG PICTURE

As a leader, you have the responsibility of assessing which elements in your church need attention. But you cannot do that alone. For one, you more-than-likely lean into one or two of them as your primary mode of operating and that's

---

[93] Acts 16:9

the paradigm by which you view your organization. In other words, you can't help but have blind spots.

A healthy process would be to have key staff and volunteers take the *Elemental Church Inventory*™. This should include your leadership and management teams and trustee or elder board and, in a creative way, those staff members or volunteers in the trenches who have expertise in the operational mechanics of their particular area, especially critical departments or ministries.

Following is a sample from the forty-eight questions in the online assessment available at *elementalinventory.com*. Once your church has registered as part of a comprehensive audit, individual leaders will take the assessment and the results are automatically collated and averaged to give you an overview score for each element. Included here as well are the online descriptions for the range of scores for each element.

Examples from the Elemental Church Inventory™

Tasks in our organization generally get done efficiently, without filling gaps at the last minute.

□*strongly disagree* □*disagree* □*neutral* □*agree* □*strongly agree*

Generally speaking, our staff members and volunteers are engaged and energized about what they are doing.

□*strongly disagree* □*disagree* □*neutral* □*agree* □*strongly agree*

We have an effective process for regular staff performance reviews.

□*strongly disagree* □*disagree* □*neutral* □*agree* □*strongly agree*

We have created a "culture of trust" in which staff and volunteers are encouraged to freely exchange ideas for improvement and new initiatives.

☐*strongly disagree* ☐*disagree* ☐*neutral* ☐*agree* ☐*strongly agree*

We take time to learn what has worked or not worked for other churches and use that information to help in our own planning.

☐*strongly disagree* ☐*disagree* ☐*neutral* ☐*agree* ☐*strongly agree*

Generally speaking, our church is not afraid to tackle challenges.

☐*strongly disagree* ☐*disagree* ☐*neutral* ☐*agree* ☐*strongly agree*

People would characterize our leadership team as open and accessible.

☐*strongly disagree* ☐*disagree* ☐*neutral* ☐*agree* ☐*strongly agree*

UNDERSTANDING YOUR CHURCH ASSESSMENT

Once your leadership team and key staff/volunteers take the online assessment, your averaged individual element scores will illuminate strengths and opportunities for your church, organization or team. The scoring will fall into four categories:

- 24 to -12: Danger

A score in this range reveals a serious deficiency. If not addressed, certain consequences will debilitate the organization and severely diminish effectiveness. Consider this: how long can an organization exist with little integrity in terms of leadership, systems or sense of mission? Or with a marginal passion for what it does and who it is? How long can it survive if it has a totally inward-focus approach, is rife with entitlement and has no sense of a greater purpose other than feeding itself? Or in our high-speed, rapidly changing world, what organization can survive without an imaginative and innovative ethos? And if more than one of the elements is in the Danger category, significant concerted action needs to be taken quickly.

-11 to 0 (zero): Caution

A score here is like the "Check Engine" light on your car's dashboard: it may or may not be a critical issue, but it certainly cannot be ignored. If it reflects a trend, the organization is in trouble. The good news is that there is a modicum of "breathing time" to develop a plan and process to address it, assuming there's not a procrastinating leadership culture in place. Though you may be able to take a "ready, aim, fire" approach, you absolutely cannot afford a "ready, aim…aim…aim…" attitude. Keep in mind that the Danger zone is just around the corner for this element.

1 to 12: Healthy

Scores in this range connote a healthy engagement with this particular element. The watchword here is "discipline": whatever system is in place to exercise this element must be guarded and maintained. It's the responsibility of leadership to be on the lookout for anything that impedes or depreciates this element in any way. Moreover, think of this element's score as a way of developing a "best-practice" template for other elements that may be flagging.

13 to 24: Thriving

This score indicates a robust implementation and flourishing of this element. Leadership should be commended on their ability to maximize the element. But like any strength, it comes with a corollary danger; it could be that the organization has made this the modus operandi. The leaders must look at the other elements to determine if any one of them has atrophied because of defaulting to this particular strength. Remember, a healthy balance of all four elements is critical for health and effectiveness.

For example, a score of "-21" (negative twenty-one) in the Passion|Fire element is a serious threat to the health of your organization. It may indicate a cancerous apathy in the most important product your organization needs: a corporate fire-in-the-belly. Or what Ken Blanchard once defined as "raving fans." Boredom, apathy, bureaucracy, politicking, a sense of entitlement, and/or infighting can all be symptoms of a lack of authentic passion for the vision and mission of the church.

Or a score of "2" in the Air|Imagination element indicates a fairly healthy culture of corporate creativity and trust. But because it's in the low end of the range, be careful to not let your foot off the gas in this area. It's easy to slip into sacred cows in methodologies and practices.

Now let's break each element down to determine what's currently needed in the team or organization you lead or are a part of.

EARTH | INTEGRITY

At its most basic level, the Earth|Integrity element can be assessed by a simple metric: is the mission of the organization being accomplished? Any healthy organization has some way of measuring its success. It may even be by benchmarking and being challenged against itself year over year. Even if accomplishment is measured in a squishier way—say, influence—there is always a way of measuring that. It is absolutely no fun to play a game and have no idea how to win. There must be a reward and outcome for our work, both personally and organizationally.[94]

But "mission accomplishment" has to be weighed against other values, such as relational and organizational health, long-term sustainability, individual worker (employee or volunteer) satisfaction, and so on. For instance, an upstart software company can have designers and engineers do lots of overnight, coffee-fueled pushes to get the product out by a deadline, but it cannot sustain that type of drive long term and year after year. No extrinsic motivation can keep someone from burning out.

In ministry, a similar drive can easily happen. One assessment that can be used is the Best Christian Workplaces survey[95] for measuring the internal health of the organization and the level of missional buy-in and engagement of the workers and volunteers.

Regardless of the tool, the only way an assessment has any value is by the degree of self-awareness the assessee has. This is where the value of a team comes into play and a broader view of reality can be determined, particularly if they've had humility and a lack of defensiveness and protectionism modeled for them.

Try starting with these questions:

Are tasks getting done that need to get done, or are you regularly filling in the gaps at the last minute to get things completed? Can you honestly say that your organizational mission is actually what everyone is focused on? Do the

---

[94] 1 Corinthians 9:24-26

[95] http://www.bcwinstitute.com

various departments or ministry areas feel connected with each other or is there a common theme of feeling siloed?

At a personal level, subtle fractures in the foundation of our individual integrity can be exposed by honestly responding to some simple questions. For instance, is there a healthy symbiosis of your work and family life?—what would your spouse say? Do you have one or two people that feel authorized to give you helpful and frank feedback at a personal level? Do you consistently feel drained and de-energized or angry and frustrated? The interplay of work and rest—both personally and organizationally—must be nurtured and balanced. Would people in your organization say they feel empowered and enjoy coming to work each day? Can your peers say that you legitimately live out the values you espouse? If you're a pastor, would the people closest to you say you honestly "practice what you preach?"

Asking questions regarding the wholeness of yourself and your organization is vital work for the elemental leader. The integration of you as a leader and the mission and processes for getting things done is of ultimate importance.

FIRE | PASSION

Is your church (or team, department, or ministry area) lagging in passion? Has a dull acceptance of the status-quo settled in? Is there a growing sense of "organizational boredom," a ho-hum approach to the mission? When was the last time your team sensed the need for a big challenge?

After less than two decades removed from World War II and facing a perceived aggressive communistic world power, America was experiencing an unprecedented economic boom, an explosion of births, and a rapidly expanding social experiment of home ownership called "the suburbs." In his

1961 inaugural address, in spite of this new prosperity, President Kennedy described the global mission of the U.S. in these terms:

> "To those peoples in the huts and villages across the globe struggling to break the bonds of mass misery, we pledge our best efforts to help them help themselves, for whatever period is required—not because the Communists may be doing it, not because we seek their votes, but because it is right. If a free society cannot help the many who are poor, it cannot save the few who are rich."

In order to accomplish this mission and to forge the New Frontier of his administration, President Kennedy then challenged average Americans to move beyond their growing affluence. He concluded his speech with the famous line, "Ask not what your country can do for you; ask what you can do for your country."

Then once again within his first one-hundred days, Kennedy recognized that in the escalating space race with the Soviet Union, something big and challenging needed to be done. He fueled passions when he raised the bar before Congress, proposing, "this nation should commit itself to achieving the goal, before this decade is out, of landing a man on the moon and returning him safely to the earth."

How long has it been since the people in your organization were challenged with something larger than themselves? When was the last time they sensed a need to sacrifice for the greater good? If people don't have anything worth dying for (at least in the figurative sense of personal sacrifice), they really don't have anything worth living for. When was the last time your people sensed that they were involved in something that was changing lives for the better?

Knowing that his mission of bringing the Kingdom to earth would be effectuated through building his ekklesia[96] (translated as *church*, but more properly a gathering of people "called out" for a specific purpose), Jesus fired up his disciples with an outrageous claim:

> *"The person who trusts me will not only do what I'm doing but even greater things, because I, on my way to the Father, am giving you the same work to do that I've been doing. You can count on it."* [97]

Can you imagine the passion—and perhaps not a small bit of terror—that those challenging words catalyzed in this ragtag group of disciples? They had been astounded and emboldened by the transrational encounters they had witnessed Jesus doing. It was so beyond the norm that the religious leaders accused him of practicing sorcery.[98] The Talmud—a collection of commentaries by Jewish scholars completed by the 5th century—mentions the man Yeshua (Jesus) who was executed "on Passover's eve for practicing sorcery and leading Israel into apostasy." The problem was not simply his moral teaching, but the powerful encounters that accompanied him and his claim to be the son of God.

Elemental leaders know that periodically their people need to be challenged with something that is beyond their abilities at an individual level.

WATER | SERVANTHOOD

Elemental leaders understand that the accomplishment of the mission is dependent on the people that they lead. They

---

[96] Matthew 16:18

[97] John 14:12 (The Message)

[98] Matthew 12:24 (New Living Translation, Second Edition)

also viscerally know their personal ambition and welfare is secondary to the organization they lead.

A true servanthood atmosphere has to be modeled, taught and clearly expressed as part of the corporate culture. It will never just happen—we human beings naturally look out for number one; it is part of our fallen nature. And, of course, our organizations will reflect our brokenness. This is where the leader must assume responsibility for the culture.

CEO Cheryl Batchelder writes bluntly,

> Some take ownership of their leadership and work to become better for the benefit of others. Some never accept responsibility and remain stuck in the spotlight. Lack of personal responsibility in a leader is just another form of self-absorption. Victim leaders revel in their difficulties and blame the rest of mankind for their troubles. By definition, this thinking blinds them to the fact that the people they serve also have troubles. Such leaders cannot serve others well until they assume personal responsibility for improving themselves and develop empathy for others.[99]

Batchelder was hired as CEO of Popeye's, a failing fast food restaurant chain. Popeye's was owned by the AFC Enterprises, who had spun off all their other acquisitions—Cinnabon, Seattle's Best Coffee, and others—to avoid bankruptcy during seven years of declining profits. In an amazing turnaround, Batchelder increased profits by forty percent with nearly three-quarters of franchise owners thrilled with a forty-four percent increase in cash flow.

She unabashedly credits the power of serving others for their remarkable turnaround. Her relentless drive to change the management culture caused them to spend untold hours

---

[99] Bachelder, Cheryl (2015-03-16). *Dare to Serve: How to Drive Superior Results by Serving Others* (pp. 144-146). Berrett-Koehler Publishers. Kindle Edition.

listening to—and learning from—their franchisees and their issues rather than forcing top-down decisions. As a matter of fact, "listening" became one of their core values.

Developing empathy became one of their primary steps to effective leadership, particularly when it came to changing a culture.

One last thought: culture is often difficult to assess, simply because it's the water we swim in. I'm sure no fish gives a second thought to being in water; it's all it knows. It's so important to get an outsider's view of your world—it's what Batchelder was when she was brought to the helm. Don't be afraid of using assessments and bringing in coaches and consultants that you trust.

AIR | IMAGINATION

Organizations have a relatively short shelf life without innovation and, oddly enough, few allot time resources to imagination and creativity. And, as with any organization, this critical element must be nurtured and promoted by the leader. Regardless of whether this is your element or not, the good news is that acquiring these necessary skills can be learned and developed. As creativity guru Ken Robinson writes:

> Aiming straight for innovation without developing the imaginative and creative powers on which it depends, would be like an athlete hoping to win a gold medal at the Olympic Games but with no intention of exercising beforehand.[100]

---

[100] Robinson, Ken (2011-06-28). *Out of Our Minds: Learning to be Creative* (Kindle Location 3775). Wiley. Kindle Edition.

Over several years, the authors of *The Innovator's DNA: Mastering the Five Skills of Disruptive Innovators*[101] interviewed hundreds of innovators and nearly five-thousand executives to distinguish the disparate ways of thinking that innovative leaders use over the average leader. The simple fact is that innovators think differently and as a result, act differently. Their surveys uncovered five key behavioral patterns:

First was their ability to practice associational thinking. They loved connecting seemingly unrelated ideas and difficulties to create new ways of thinking. Innovators never seemed to shy away from uncovering other organizations and people who had solved similar problems, often simply asking if someone else had already come up with a solution.

Second, they tended to be keen observers. For instance, it has long been known that the cleverest comedians are typically good at observing—and interpreting with humor—the unique foibles of humans and even their own responses to life's circumstances. Likewise, imaginative leaders seem to have a heightened sense of "noticing" and then taking the time to interpret their observations.

Third, observation led to the practice of questioning why, as in why we or others do this or that.

Fourth, innovators practice networking with a diversity of people. They see their interaction with people of various backgrounds as a way of garnering new understandings.

Last, imaginative leaders experiment. They typically don't want to wait for data; instead, they want to make data! Experimentation allows for the creation of new data points.

---

[101] Jeff Dyer, Hal Gregersen, Clayton M. Christensen; *The Innovator's DNA: Mastering the Five Skills of Disruptive Innovators* (Boston, Harvard Business School Publishing, 2011)

At an organizational level, how are those five practices being developed in your leaders? If there seems to be a dearth of these practices, you have just discovered your primary way of assessing the strength of the Air|Imagination element.

If you're a church leader, please don't dismiss this as mere "corporate-speak"; a cursory reading of the gospels reveals what an imaginative and innovative rabbi Jesus was. His observations and revolutionary strategies seriously upset the religious establishment and status quo. His seemingly relentless questions posed to his followers caused them to think differently. His miraculous handling of the fish and loaves to feed thousands of people certainly tapped into "new technologies to serve people better!" That "approach" would have never been considered by the political and religious powers of that day.

Elemental leaders intuitively know that the Air | Imagination element is crucial, but often the busy-ness of management crowd it out. The truth is: no future-oriented organization can afford to overlook it.

ELEMENTAL CHURCH MATRIX

EARTH
Integrity

Strong systems, good communication and drive for mission, but may feel top-down controlling. Status quo may not allow for creativity and innovation.

FIRE
Passion

Solid organizational character, but may be suffering from malaise and stagnant ideas. No real excitement about the future.

ORGANIZATIONAL SWEETSPOT

No shortage of ideas and entrepreneurial thinking, but major frustration with entitlement issues, communication, and processes.

WATER
Servanthood

Humble leadership and staff. Very creative culture, but can have difficulty getting things done. Clear direction and clarified decision-making may be needed.

AIR
Imagination

CHAPTER 8
MOVING FORWARD

*But regarding anything beyond this, dear friend, go easy.
There's no end to the publishing of books, and constant study
wears you out so you're no good for anything else.*

~ECCLESIASTES 12:12 (THE MESSAGE)

The previous chapter-page quote is from the book of Ecclesiastes in the Bible. Take your medication before reading: the author is painfully honest about the seemingly randomness and pain of life as he questions its very meaning. It is not for the fainthearted.

But there is a reality-check in this simple verse: more than likely, this isn't the first leadership book you've read. And it probably won't be the last. Most good leaders want to develop themselves as best they can, whether that be attending conferences, seeking mentors, reading books, taking assessments, rubbing shoulders with other leaders, and so on. But like everything else in life, it doesn't mean anything without application. I can read and study until I'm blue in the face, but the first step toward effective leadership is simply asking the question: what am I going to do about it?

In any organization, it's vitally important to use the same language. I would hope with whatever team you lead, each person would read through the material and take the time to actively discuss the reflection points in chapters two through five.

But the real work comes with your personal and organizational assessments. For the *Elemental Leader Personal Assessment* ™, take the time to invite the rest of your team to weigh in on the results: do they affirm that "you're in your element"? Create space for each team member to share their primary element and appraise where there may be "element gaps" in your team. If there is a disparity, what might you do to balance that out?—are there other staff members with that key element that can be called on for input from time-to-time, perhaps in the preplanning stages of a particular project or strategy?

Next, if you opted for an audit, discuss the results of the *Elemental Church Inventory* ™. This is best done in a leadership/management team retreat. Taking the time to discuss the scores in a setting that's free from everyday work distractions is critical. It's good to reflect on why a particular element, say, the Fire|Passion element, is strong in your context—consider why that is and whether any "best practices" should be jealously protected or replicated in some way. Is it reflective of the "elemental makeup" of the leadership team? Or vice-versa, if an element is weak, what strategies can be uniquely used in your organization to enhance it? Make the strengthening of that element a key strategic focus over the next year as well as revisit the reflection points in chapters two through five from an organizational standpoint.

CLOSING...AND A PERSONAL PASTORAL OBSERVATION

Over the years I've found myself ruminating on why pastors are often reluctant to engage with outside organizational assessors, auditors, and coaches or even in-house team-based reviews and surveys. I think it's the human condition in general that makes us reluctant to expose our weaknesses or fear of change in front of others. Over decades of pastoring, I watched a somewhat similar dynamic with marriages that were going south. After finally recognizing the need for marriage counseling, stereotypically it was often the husband who dragged his feet into my office; after all, what self-respecting man wants to admit in front of another man that he's having trouble doing something that he thinks he's supposed to already know how to do?

In dysfunctional settings where perhaps a board and senior pastor are at odds, or a "culture of honor" and trust have not been established with staff, it's inevitable that a leader feels he or she must carefully guard their vulnerabilities. But the trouble is, we all have our blind spots—both personally and organizationally—and unless we take the time to amp up our level of self-awareness and our organizational discernment, we risk limiting the scope of our influence.

As I referenced in chapter two, Jesus demands that his followers become reflective when it comes to personal perception when he says,

> *"Why do you notice the little piece of dust in your friend's eye, but you don't notice the big piece of wood in your own eye? How can you say to your friend, 'Let me take that little piece of dust out of your eye'? Look at yourself! You still have that big piece of wood in your own eye. You hypocrite! First, take the wood out of your own eye. Then you will see clearly to take the dust out of your friend's eye."* [102]

This is a leadership issue because he's talking about the need to help others to discover the things that cause them pain or limit their ability to see their world effectively or function at the peak of their ability. But it first requires a high degree of self-leadership.

Then in challenging his followers on the cost of discipleship, Jesus employs a metaphor that implies a principle of organizational self-awareness:

> *"Suppose one of you wants to build a tower. Will he not first sit down and estimate the cost to see if he has enough money to complete it? For if he lays the foundation and is not*

---

[102] Matthew 7:3-5 (New Century Version)

able to finish it, everyone who sees it will ridicule him, saying, 'This fellow began to build and was not able to finish. '"[103]

While focusing his followers on personal discipleship, Jesus uses an example of organizational discernment. Our churches, ministries, and organizations must be aware of their own limitations and Achilles' heels as well as their barrier-breaking potential and scope.

The people you lead and the world your church or ministry has the opportunity to influence and transform deserve the best...and no organization can flourish long-term without the four foundational elements: Integrity, Passion, Servanthood, and Imagination.

My deepest hope is that you bring out the best and highest capabilities in the people you are privileged to lead. And all for the Kingdom.

For more resources and leadership development tools, visit www.elementalchurches.com

---

[103] Luke 14:28-30

THE ELEMENTAL CHURCHES INVENTORY

The *Elemental Churches Inventory* combines personalized coaching with a self-guided, team-based learning experience designed to increase organizational self-awareness and health in four critical areas: Integrity (systems), Passion (commitment), Servanthood (outward-focus), and Imagination (innovation). The system merges personal and group learning and reflection with external analysis to produce personalized action plans focused on your unique context.

THE BACKSTORY

After pastoring for thirty years and stepping down from leading the Vineyard Cincinnati Church, author, speaker, and mentor Dave Workman formed a team to create a system for church leaders to develop more organizational discernment regarding the health and potential of their churches. Using his book *Elemental Leaders* along with the exercises, surveys, and assessments in the accompanying *Elemental Churches Field Guide* by Dr. Tom Thatcher, they combined self-discovery with outside data-driven analysis. The Elemental Churches team believes that with the right tools, pastors can take their own staff and key volunteers through a team-based, self-guided organizational-development curriculum and find it not only transformational, but cost-efficient as well.

The *Elemental Churches Inventory* guides your leadership team through a thorough review of church health in dialogue with the Elemental Churches coaches as you upload data and assessments online at the *elementalinventory.com* website with your church login. They analyze your data from staff interviews and key information surveys, as well as observing your weekend services, environments, and listening to your leadership challenges. Their observations, and yours, will lead to a concise yet detailed report on your church, with specific action steps.

TEST DRIVE

Check out more info at *www.elementalinventory.com*. On the website, you can take a free *Elemental Leaders Personal Assessment* and watch a video on how the *Elemental Churches Inventory* works. The complete kit includes 12 *Elemental Leaders* books, 12 *Elemental Churches Field Guides* (a 70-page workbook), 16 online videos, multiple surveys and assessments, staff interviews, phone consults, and a final comprehensive report.

ELEMENTAL CHURCHES

SEE OUR TOOLBOX 🧰 AT ELEMENTALCHURCHES.COM

FOCUS is a revolutionary strategic-planning-in-a-box experience for your church leadership team. Carefully designed to be self-facilitating, your team will go through a six-hour "game-like" process with highly interactive exercises to create a 12-to-24 month master plan for moving your church forward. Strategic team-based planning has never been more comprehensive, energizing, and, believe it or not, fun! **For more info including a quick video of how FOCUS works, click here.**

ORDER INFO

VIBE is a team experience designed to make your church more inviting and effective in reaching new people. Through a series of assessments and group exercises, team members take on the role of a "secret shopper" to view everything from your church service to facilities to the variety of ministries offered on a weekend to your website. Everything changes when you view your church through the lens of a "new person" visiting for the first time. **Check out a quick 2-minute video overview here.**

ORDER INFO

The ELEMENTARY CHURCHES INVENTORY is a unique web-based assessment to measure church health and effectiveness. Combining individual and team learning through online surveys and videos with personalized coaching, the Inventory provides a comprehensive report with action steps. It's a roadmap based on your own uploaded reports and surveys as you and your team work through the personal and group exercises. For more info and pricing, visit www.elemental-inventory.com.

INVENTORY WEBSITE

The ELEMENTAL CHURCHES SELF-GUIDED INVENTORY is the little brother to the EC INVENTORY. In this version, leadership teams work through all the same leadership development exercises and videos, but without the comprehensive analysis and report presentation at the end. But that's not short-changing the learnings your team will experience in the personal and group reflective exercises. Because of less "hand-holding" from a face-to-face consultant, we can offer it at a fraction of the price.

ORDER INFO

If you already have the FOCUS Strategy Tool but are ready to do another round of strategic planning with your team, save some serious money by simply ordering the FOCUS Refill Kit. Each kit comes with 1 FOCUS GO!Pad, 36 Opportunity Sheets, 4 Goal Circle Cards, 16 Strategy Circle Cards, 16 Champion Circle Cards, 4 Brainstorm Sheets, 12 Prayer Journals, 1 Game Plan Sheet, 16 Champion Tokens, and 48 Stickers. New to the FOCUS Strategic Planning Tool? Visit FocusStrategyGame.com for info!

ORDER INFO

NEED IN-DEPTH CONSULTING?
Sometimes "stuck" churches need specific hands-on help with unique problems. For basic retainer fees, we offer full access to our decades of church leadership experience. And for a one-on-one personal touch, we provide coaching to pastors for less than you spend on your cable bill. Seriously. We want to coach you through your challenges with practical advice, resources, and prayer. Call 513.400.4595 or email info@partnershipadvisors.com.

MORE INFO

RENEW fills a unique niche in the leader's toolbox. Renew contains everything you need for a leadership team spiritual retreat...designed solely to bring refreshment and renewal to tired teams. The interactive exercises and quiet times with Jesus are specially designed to fit into any denominational or non-denom context. With both team interaction and individual reflection, your team is guaranteed to leave this one-day retreat material with renewed gratitude and passion for the Kingdom.

ORDER INFO

ENVISION is a highly interactive, gamified process for unlocking the vision and mission God has given your church. Whether you're churchplanting or struggling with vision-drift, envision guides leadership teams in discovering and clarifying God's purposes. With probing questions and exercises, your team will develop a unified vision statement, a defined list of core values, marching orders that are unique to your church, and a vibrant picture of who God wants you to be in your your context.

ORDER INFO

Made in the USA
Monee, IL
28 February 2020

22379571R00115